SPEECH CORRECTION AT HOME

Speech Correction
—At Home

By

MORRIS VAL JONES, Ph.D.

Director, Speech and Reading Clinic
Morrison Center for Rehabilitation
Instructor in Speech, Golden Gate College
San Francisco, California

Foreword by

HERBERT C. MOFFITT, JR., M.D.

Chairman, Medical Advisory Committee
Morrison Center for Rehabilitation
San Francisco, California

CHARLES C THOMAS • PUBLISHER
Springfield • Illinois • U.S.A.

CHARLES C THOMAS • PUBLISHER

BANNERSTONE HOUSE

301-327 East Lawrence Avenue, Springfield, Illinois, U.S.A.

Published simultaneously in the British Commonwealth of Nations by

BLACKWELL SCIENTIFIC PUBLICATIONS, LTD., OXFORD, ENGLAND

Published simultaneously in Canada by

THE RYERSON PRESS, TORONTO

Copyright 1957, by CHARLES C THOMAS • PUBLISHER

Library of Congress Catalog Card Number: 56-11484

Printed in the United States of America

To

Laurie

Stanley

and

Craig

FOREWORD

In recent years there has been an increasing tendency for specialization within the medical profession. As this field of knowledge has expanded, it has become ever more difficult for the physician adequately to master all aspects of his vocation and he has come to depend on his associates for help in their particular specialties. At times, the practitioner of medicine will even call upon a whole team of expert specialists such as is now available in the major centers of population. Of these, we in San Francisco are fortunate in having a group primarily concerned with rehabilitation at the May T. Morrison Center.

Many patients and their physicians, however, cannot avail themselves of the services of a group of experts, nor even a single expert in speech therapy. While we are becoming more aware of the problems of oral communication and the need for specialized guidance, we do not always find such instruction available. "Speech Correction at Home" fills a definite need. It will be a guide to the parents and teachers of children with speech problems, to adult stutterers, and to those responsible for the care of stroke victims and laryngectomized patients. The first chapter, on speech development, can prove helpful to every parent.

This book should also be a valued aid for every physician who needs assistance in the treatment of those with speech problems. It is a readily available reference source for pediatricians and mental hygienists.

HERBERT C. MOFFITT, JR., M.D.

INTRODUCTION

Speech Correction at Home presents in simple non-technical language selected information concerning speech problems. It tells how friends and family members may help persons with trouble in oral communication to overcome their handicap. In the case of adults many of the suggestions may be carried out by the patients themselves. The material is drawn from the practical experiences of a speech therapist who has been employed in both public schools and private clinics.

Each chapter deals with the speech problems which might confront any family. Besides giving directions for the care of the speech patient, the author summarizes briefly his convictions about aspects of speech re-education. At the end of each chapter he gives a list of published materials which will supply additional information; practice exercises appear in the Appendix.

This book is not intended to replace the speech therapist. Consultation with the specialist in speech correction is desirable in every case. With severely involved cases the guidance of a professionally trained therapist is essential.

This presentation is intended primarily for the untrained parent, wife, or friend who becomes the helper of a speech-handicapped individual. It would be a useful reference for dentists, orthodontists, and doctors: general practitioners, pediatricians, and otolaryngologists. Teachers, counselors, and clergymen will find directive materials which may be passed along to persons with speech problems or to those who are trying to help them. Students in speech therapy and in special education courses might find the suggestions and illustrations serviceable in their clinical practice.

Sources of information about speech therapists:

1. American Speech and Hearing Association
   George A. Kopp, Ph.D., Secretary-Treasurer
   Wayne University
   Detroit, Michigan
2. The National Society for Crippled Children and Adults, Inc.
   11 S. La Salle Street
   Chicago, Illinois
3. County Medical Association
4. Local school authorities

ACKNOWLEDGMENTS

The following persons read parts of the manuscript and offered suggestions for its improvement. Errors, of course, remain the fault of the author.

Anderson, Virgil A., Ph.D., Director, Speech and Hearing Clinic, Stanford University, California

Jackson, Mrs. Ruth Montgomery, Consultant, Speech Education, Palo Alto Unified School District, Palo Alto, California (Chapter I)

Kellogg, Mrs. Rhoda, Supervisor, Golden Gate Nursery Schools, San Francisco, California (Chapter II)

Rasmus, Ward, Ph.D., Director, Speech and Hearing Center, San Jose State College, California (Chapter III)

Morrison, Lewis F., M.D., Otolaryngologist, San Francisco, California (Chapter V)

Schiller, Francis, M.D., Department of Neurology, Kaiser Foundation Hospital, San Francisco, California (Chapter VI)

Wedberg, Conrad, Consultant in Speech Correction, State Department of Education, Sacramento, California (Chapter IV)

M. V. J.

CONTENTS

SPEECH CORRECTION AT HOME

CHAPTER I

YOUR CHILD LEARNS TO TALK

To: Parents of pre-school children

Y our child is now six months old. He is cooing, singing, and making any number of assorted noises. In the babbling stage of speech development, he is trying on—or trying out—a multitude of sounds, speech sounds. Some of them happen to be in the English language; most of them do not. Later he will discard those which fail to gain results in talking with other people, those which do not fit into the language pattern of his family.

SPEECH DEVELOPS SLOWLY

Let's look ahead a few years. At five, your child will have a vocabulary of approximately two thousand words. He will be able to express himself in full sentences, using reasonably correct grammar. His oral communication will reflect the vocabulary and language forms of his immediate family. He will have learned speech by imitating what he has heard.

Two ideas in that last sentence need expanding. The child learns from what he hears. Speech is not an instinctive, inborn quality; it is a learned activity.

You, as parents (and particularly the mother), provide a model which the child hears and copies. We know that he cannot read; so his total vocabulary consists of words which he hears from you, his friends, and the radio and television.

Learning to speak is a difficult task. It may be learned poorly or well. It may be learned spontaneously with little direct attention paid to it. You may occasionally correct a pronunciation, or straighten out a grammatical form: "Billy, we say 'I threw the ball' and not 'I throwed the ball.'" Or the learning of speech may require years of special exercises and extensive training in such cases as cleft palate or cerebral palsy. In this chapter, we shall consider only the normal development of speech.

1

A. Pre-Speech Is Important

The child has a natural drive to express himself orally. When he is only a month old, he will, if stimulated by the active interest of his parents, respond to speech. After a considerable amount of wrestling with himself, including excited panting, he may emit a barely audible gurgle. As you continue to talk with him many times a day, he will amplify his responses. He will laugh, as he enjoys talking things over with you. You may encourage him by saying, "Talk about it"; "Tell

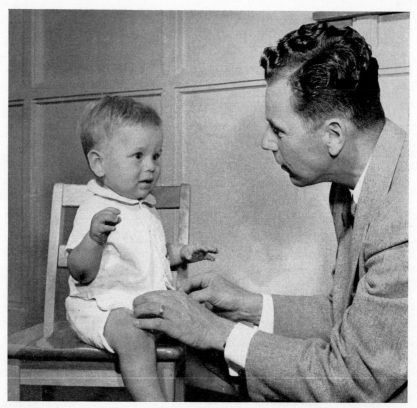

Courtesy of Morrison Center for Rehabilitation.

Fig. 1. "Come on, Boy, let's talk about it."

Mommy all about it"; "Come on, Boy, let's talk it over." This babbling stage of speech development begins about the end of the second month and continues for four or five months. It will overlap with succeeding phases of speech development, but it is most prominent in the latter part of his first six months.

At about seven months, the child will begin to reproduce the sounds which are directed to him by his mother, father, and other members of the family. He is less likely to respond to strangers, but some babies are naturally friendly and will do so. The first sounds to be echoed are the vowels in isolation, as "oo," "oh," "ah." These and other vowels form his language for a few weeks. You will gain more response from him if you speak to him using isolated vowel sounds rather than a whole complex of language. He may gain comfort and a feeling of love and affection from speech. But if you are trying for vocal response on his part, stick to "oo," "ah," "ee" and other vowel sounds.

Within a few weeks he will begin to add consonant sounds. The first of these to appear will probably be the lip sounds, "p" and "b," and the nasal sounds, "m" and "n." Soon afterwards, "t" and "d" will appear. Along about this time, in the seventh or eighth month, you may be fooled into thinking he is actually saying words. Because of his ability to echo what he hears, he may reproduce some word with which he has been stimulated. "Mama" or "Dada" are the usual ones. But, poor dear, he doesn't know what he is saying. He is pleased, of course, with the applause and the added attention and will probably continue to perform by echoing such simple words which contain sounds within his repertoire.

B. The Child Uses Real Speech

Purposive speech, that is, words produced with the intention of expressing an idea—or of controlling the environment, will probably not occur until the eleventh or twelfth month *or later*. Now he usually begins to use a single word of one syllable, such as "go," "bye," or "me." "Mama" is used for the express purpose of attracting the attention of the female parent. The child is beginning to feel his power in controlling his surroundings. Other single words, including those with two repeated syllables, as "Dada," are added to the vocabulary. One word is often used to express an entire sentence: "Go?" "Cookie," or "More." These one-word sentences may satisfy his need for speech for several months.

A slowing down of vocabulary building may occur while the child learns to walk. It is too much for him to learn two things at once. In fact, he may almost stop talking for a while as he concentrates his efforts on this new skill. But by the end of another six months, two-word sentences ("I do," "Me want," etc.) appear.

After the age of eighteen months, speech begins to blossom forth. The child discards many of the sounds which serve no purpose in expressing his desires. He perfects those sounds which are rewarded by bringing about action from his associates, mainly his parents. Even though he continues to mispronounce many of his words and uses mutilated sentences, his speech is intelligible. He is unaware that his speech is different from that of other people in his immediate environment. By the time he reaches kindergarten, his speech has achieved adult form. The vocabulary remains limited and there may be difficulty with grammar, but language patterns are well developed.

C. Responsibility for Speech Lies with the Parents

The development of normal speech is in the hands of the family. You, probably untrained in speech teaching methods, are responsible for the speech habits of your children. That does not mean that you are necessarily to blame if they do not develop normal speech. However, if there is no physical cause for faulty speech, you would do well to examine closely your part in this complicated process of learning oral communication. Whether you want to be a teacher or not, the fact remains that you are. You are doing a good, bad, or indifferent job of it.

The remainder of this chapter will suggest ways in which you can encourage the speech and language development of your child. You will be spending a great deal of time with the child; so it is better that you do those things which will help, not hinder, his speech development. By knowing what to do and what not to do, you can avoid some of the attitudes and actions which contribute to the making of several million speech-defective children in this country. It is estimated that at least five percent of the school population have speech problems. Something has gone wrong somewhere.

PARENTS CAN HELP IN SPECIFIC WAYS

By understanding the stages of speech development, you can help to prevent speech problems. In the child's first months you can "talk" to him and establish a sense of communication. The noisy baby—full of happy noises—is more likely to develop adequate speech than the quiet, passive one. Keep the baby, during his waking hours, in the center of the family's activities so that he can watch and react to what goes on. Take time out to bring him into the conversation. From the earliest months make him feel an important member of the family unit.

A. Let Him Babble

When the baby starts to babble, give him plenty of time to express himself. Don't interrupt his efforts to try out the hundreds of sounds which his articulatory equipment—mouth, lips, tongue—is able to make. He is warming up, as an orchestra tunes up, for future speech activities. This babbling period is extremely important as a step on the way toward purposive speech. If the child is prevented from carrying on his vocal play, true speech is likely to be delayed. When you speak to the child, use his language. That is, listen to what sounds he is making and then repeat them back to him. "Gli, gli, gu, gu" is preferable to a full adult sentence.

B. Be a Good Speech Model

Later, when the child begins to use actual words, the effort must be made to provide him with a correct model. Insofar as you can understand him, repeat the words he intended to use. *Avoid any baby talk.*

You may encourage communication by getting him to imitate your gestures. And when you use words, accompany them with gestures to be sure that he understands what you mean. At all times, give him plenty of time to respond either with gestures or with words. His timing apparatus may be entirely different from yours, and it is frustrating to be hurried. When the child is a little older, he will say, "Wait a minute. Just a minute," and then take the time he needs to tell his story.

At the beginning of language, the child may use an abbreviated word or even a substitute. These invented words will grow and change into real words if the child is not pushed. You may use the correct name for an object, but at the same time accept the child's term. For example, he may say "wa" when he wants a drink. You may respond, "Oh, water. Yes. Mommy will get you some water." Avoid "Don't say 'wa'; it's 'water.'" "Ga" may change into "gatten," then to "botten," and finally to "bottle." Other short forms and substitution will also grow into words which are normally part of the English language.

Girls, on the average, speak earlier and more distinctly than boys. Speech scientists have failed to discover why this should be so. But girls mature more quickly in the language skills. This tendency carries on through the elementary school and includes reading, writing, and spelling. If you understand this fact, you will not expect your boy to speak as clearly as a girl of the same age. Boys are more numerous among the speech-defective group than girls, and among stutterers the ratio is eight or more boys to every girl.

C. Encourage Him to Talk

You can make sure that your home provides an environment which will stimulate speech. Accept the child as a member of the family group who has a right to express his opinions and to contribute to the family discussion. Even before the age of two, he should be encouraged to speak as much as possible, even though only about half of what he says is intelligible. If he fails to find a word, you can help him by supplying it. Give him time to search before you step in with this assistance. This help can be disguised as interest and stated in such a way that he is unaware that he is being helped.

You should encourage the child to speak. Don't go too far with the attitude so often expressed, "Oh, he'll talk when he's ready." There is a speech readiness age during which the child is more easily stimulated toward speech. When this period, usually from a year and a half to two and a half years of age, is allowed to pass, speech development becomes much more difficult. If the child has made no attempt to speak meaningful words by the time he is two and a half years old, you should investigate possible causes for the delay. Many of these causes will be discussed in Chapter II.

It is important to stimulate the child toward speech when he is in a good mood. Speech is most likely to occur spontaneously as a part of play activity or some happy occupation. Also speech will come more easily as a part of an activity rather than as a mere parroting. In trying for words, choose those which contain the easier sounds— those near the beginning of the series in the Appendix. He is more apt to say "ball" than "scissors."

Be cautious about understanding too much of the child's incoherent mumblings. If he can get by with little effort, he may fail to attempt better speech. Parents often handicap the child by interpreting for him; older sisters and brothers often do this also. Unless the child is forced to realize that he must speak as others in his environment, he may get by with assorted grunts and groans and a handful of words. Although you should avoid scolding this child, you can suggest a word for him and insist that he make an attempt to use it.

D. Surround Him with Speech Stimulation

Since the child learns his speech from his immediate environment, you are in a position to control what he hears to some extent. You can be sure that your speech is correct and a good model for him to follow. Speak slowly and clearly. Avoid too many words and too long and involved sentences. You can make the child alert to sound by saying, whenever sounds or noises occur, "What was that?" It may be an airplane, a fire engine, or a truck. The whistle of a train, the bark of a dog, or the crowing of a rooster may be utilized in this ear-training program.

A very useful language-building device is asking the child to carry out directions. At first you will ask him to do only one thing, such as close the door or bring a book. A child of two years may be at this stage of development. As the memory improves, partly through the growth of the child and partly through your training, you may make the oral directions more complicated. Ask a child of four that two or even three things be done—for example: "Close the door, take off your sweater, and then wash your hands." Directions of a more complicated nature may be introduced to a child of five or so to check auditory memory and the ability to interpret oral language. "Mary, in the middle drawer of Mommy's dresser is a box. Look in it and bring me the little box with the white buttons." In like manner, words such as "under," "on," "beside," and "between" may be taught.

E. Have a Story Hour

A part of the program for language development is a regular story hour—or story time, perhaps only ten or fifteen minutes. You may find that bedtime is the best and easiest hour to remember to tell the story. Interest in books cannot begin too young. It forms a basis for later enthusiasm for reading and eventually builds into academic success in high school and college. You, the parent, must have a genuine interest in books for your child and as much as possible enjoy them with him. "Let's read a story" is much better than "Look at your books, dear." The child loves to share the book and to discuss it as you read it to him. Expect frequent interruptions and the introduction of extraneous material. These side issues may be as important to the child as the story itself.

Courtesy of Morrison Center for Rehabilitation.

Fig. 2. Story time is a "must" for every home.

Let the child have a bookcase in his room. Some books of his own plus library books should be available to him. Then at bedtime he may select the one already heard many times, or he may choose "the new one from the library." By the time he is two years old or so, you and your child should look forward to the story as well as the pictures at reading time. A good book to start with is "Mother Goose"; many other worthwhile books are available at the grocery store book rack. Many times you must simplify the language—or tell the story in your own words. Most important is that the child enjoys the story hour.

F. Use Phonograph Records

Other commercial audio-visual aids may be employed in the listening training program. There are many excellent records on the market. Of special help is "Muffin in the Country," which tells of the sounds a little dog hears when he visits a farm. A companion record is "Muffin in the City." Radio and television programs can be selected to encourage the child to listen carefully and to relate what he has heard. Just a word of caution: with the very young child it is important to avoid mutilated speech, whether it is baby talk, regional speech, or foreign accent. After his speech patterns are well established, occasional listening to such records, radio or television programs will probably do no harm. After the babbling stage, the parents and others in the child's environment should provide worthy speech models.

G. Buy Toys Wisely

Toys are useful in stimulating speech. Some parents are happy to report that the child will amuse himself quietly for hours. This may be good for concentration, but it hardly contributes to speech development. Many speech-provoking toys and games are available on the market. Among them are the various types of "Lotto," such as "Good Things to Eat Lotto," "Things that Go Lotto," and "Zoo Lotto." Less complicated games are "Chicken in the Coop" and "Peek-a-Boo." Puppets and toy telephones call for speech activities. Play acting or dressing up as a cowboy or space man may help the shy child to develop speech in a less realistic and therefore less frightening atmosphere. Puzzles are good if you help in putting them together and talk to him in the process. "Where does this piece go?" "Do you think this piece will go here?" Again, "Let's work a puzzle" is better than "Go play with your toys."

Courtesy of Golden Gate Nursery Schools.

Fig. 3. Proper toys for each age level are important.

H. Help the Child Gain Experience

The child cannot talk much if he has nothing to talk about. You can help him build up a background of experiences. Take him to the zoo, to the park, to the grocery store, and to the beach. Field trips do not need to be long or expensive. It is important that you discuss the trip with him before, during, and after it occurs. A camping trip may provide bits of conversation for several weeks or even months.

Association with children of his own age is very important. Brothers and sisters are not always the best companions because of the difference in age. Or the speech of a younger child may be too imperfect to help. Attendance at a well-run nursery school at the age of three is excellent. Help the child in every way possible to increase the limits of his knowledge. Take his questions seriously even though many of them appear to be attention-getting devices.

I. Permit the Child to Grow Up

The speech of the child is a reflection of his general level of maturation. He must not only grow, but he must grow up. His speech development can be encouraged indirectly by permitting and, to a certain extent, forcing him to become more mature. Part of the process is making him aware that he is a big boy and that you are proud to have such a helper around. By checking with books on child development, you can ascertain what activities he should be participating in at his age and encourage him to do so. The answer may lie in part in your doing less for him and making him do more for himself. Let him know that you expect intelligible speech from him; see that he is not rewarded for behavior, including speech, which is immature for his age. Although he must not be compared unfavorably with other children, he can be stimulated to want to act his true age. Unless there are complicating physical or emotional factors, when he takes more grown-up attitudes toward himself and his associates, his speech will reflect this new-found maturity.

The best basis for normal speech development is a home in which the child feels secure and loved. If you are parents who love and respect each other, you have the makings of such a home. Your family circle is a little island in a hostile world so far as the child is concerned. No child can reach forth eagerly to the community until he has solved the problems of relations with the members of his family. If his efforts to do so consume too much of his time and energy, he is too tired or preoccupied to carry on successfully outside the home at school or on the playground. The home must provide a firm base from which he can explore a shaky and uncertain world.

J. Provide Outside Contacts

You can help the child make the transition from home to the community. Invite friends in, both yours and his, so that he gets accustomed to meeting children and adults. Teach him the proper way to acknowledge introductions; show him, by example, how to greet people warmly. Although he must learn to make friends without your help, a little maneuvering on your part may make the going a bit

Courtesy of Golden Gate Nursery Schools.

Fig. 4. "We want ice cream now."

easier. Attendance at Sunday school has its social as well as religious values, and it is an easy and natural step to take. The fact that it comes once each week and lasts only an hour makes it ideal for the first out-of-home experience. Later, around the age of three, two or three mornings per week at nursery school will enlarge his contacts and give him additional controlled language experiences and learning activities. By the time he is ready for kindergarten, he will have adequate oral language to enter the classroom with confidence. He will have an excellent send-off for the many years of academic life.

SUMMARY

Speech is the most complicated achievement of mankind; speech sets him apart from all other members of the animal kingdom. The newborn baby is unable to communicate by differentiated sounds. His learning process follows an orderly sequence: (1) the birth cry, (2) babbling, (3) echoing, (4) interpreting the speech of others, and (5) purposive speech. Real speech begins about the age of one year and includes three stages: (a) single words, usually beginning with names of things, (b) the two-word sentence, and (c) complete sentences. Through listening to the speech about him, he learns to carry on oral communication with individuals in his personal world. Children vary in their time of learning speech; girls usually develop oral language sooner than boys.

You parents are responsible for the language development of your children. You may need help from specialists, such as speech therapists, psychologists, and family counselors. Although nursery schools and other agencies may aid your children in their language development, you provide the speech models and the stimulation for accomplishment. By understanding the stages of language development, you are better able to assist your child to enjoy and develop to the fullest each succeeding phase. You will know when and how to stimulate speech production. You will know what standards to set for reasonable achievement.

You, as the mature parent, will accept your child as he is and lead him to further accomplishment. By so doing, you will indirectly develop his ability to express himself orally. In addition to providing an extensive background of experience upon which to base conversations, you will set the stage in the home to encourage language development through speech-stimulating games, toys, and books. By your interest and participation with the child, you will let him know at all times that he is loved and wanted. If your child is to win success in the world outside the home, the way can be made easier when he has acceptable relationships with members of his own family. Then, too, you can help him bridge the gap between the home and out-of-home activities, which may begin with Sunday school, nursery school and the neighborhood playground.

BOOKS TO READ

ANDERSON, VIRGIL A.: *Improving the Child's Speech.* New York, Oxford University Press, 1953.

JOHNSON, WENDELL (Editor): *Speech Problems of Children.* New York, Grune and Stratton, 1950, chaps. I and II.

VAN RIPER, CHARLES: *Teaching Your Child to Talk.* New York, Harper and Brothers, 1950.

CHAPTER II

IF YOUR CHILD CAN'T TALK

To: The parents of the four-year old whose speech is
    difficult to understand.

Far too many children fail to develop speech in the manner described in Chapter I. The speech of approximately fifteen per cent
of four-year-old children is difficult to comprehend, especially for
persons outside their family circles. In about five per cent of these
cases physical factors, such as cleft palate or cerebral palsy, account
in part for their lack of speech development. Another two per cent
have low mentality, which is a deterrent to adequate speech.

But what of the remaining eight percent or so who have no physical defects and whose intelligence is normal or above? By four years
of age the normal child should be able to express himself intelligibly
in complete sentences upon any subject within his experience. Although he may have two or three sound substitutions, such as "w"
for "r" and "f" for "th," he should have no difficulty in making his
desires known to his family, his friends, and even to strangers.

TYPES OF FAULTY SPEECH

Children may show one or more of the following types of faulty
speech.

A. Lack of Quantity

These children speak very little. In extreme cases they may use
only a dozen words or less in attempting oral communication. Such a
vocabulary is inadequate, of course, and must be supplemented by
grunts, groans, and various gestures. John, age 4, is such a child. He
says "Mama," "go," "bye-bye," and "bow-wow," and that is all. His
parents, particularly his mother, may have become adept at interpreting his gesture language, but other adults and children are at a complete loss with him. Carol, age 3½, has a few more words in her

15

vocabulary, but she does not use sentences. Sometimes she puts two words together, such as "No want" or "Me go." The words which John and Carol speak are clear, but they just do not use enough of them. Oral communication is limited in the extreme.

B. Faulty Pronunciation

These children speak as much as other children of their age, but many of their words are incorrectly pronounced. Joe, just turned 4, speaks at great length on a number of subjects, but no one can understand him. Even his parents are at a loss most of the time. The out-of-family listener might recognize an occasional word, but for the most part, Joe might as well be speaking a foreign language. Examples of his speech are presented (with translation):

"Ee id doin' dow a teet."—He is going down the street.

"I taw a wid mou wun in at oom."—I saw a little mouse run into that room.

C. Lack of Fluency (Stuttering)

These children may show characteristics of the first two classifications, but the outstanding fault of their speech is stumbling over words. They repeat the initial consonant of a word, hold onto the vowel, or repeat entire words or phrases. They have sufficient difficulty so that people are aware that they have trouble in speaking. By this time—age 4—someone has remarked to them about the difficulty. Their worried parents have asked the family doctor about it. He may have said, "Oh, they grow out of it," but so far they have not.

Although the suggestions of this chapter are applicable to stuttering children, more detail about this problem will be given in Chapter IV.

FINDING THE CAUSE

The first step in helping the four-year old with delayed speech is to search for causal factors. Why hasn't he followed the normal speech development pattern? If he has an obvious physical defect, such as cleft palate, the help of a trained speech therapist may be needed. Although the major portion of the speech training will remain the task of the family, the therapist can guide the program and give suggestions.

A. Hearing

Does the child hear well? Since speech development is dependent upon hearing the speech of others, a hearing loss may be responsible for the lack of acquisition of speech sounds, particularly the high pitched sounds, such as "s" and "f." If the child is cooperative, he

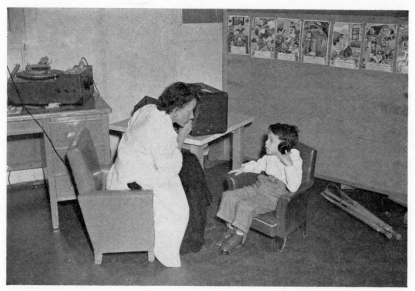

Courtesy of School for Cerebral Palsied Children, Northern California.

Fig. 5. How well the child hears is essential information for the speech teacher.

can be tested with an audiometer and an approximate audiogram (picture of his hearing) be obtained. If he lacks sufficient language to take the necessary directions, he may need to be tested by more indirect and complicated procedures. In any case, a watch tick test is not enough to determine if a hearing loss is causing his lack of speech development.

B. Intelligence

What of the child's intelligence? There is no doubt that, in general, speech development and intelligence are closely related. If the child does not respond to language stimulation, the need for a psychometric test is indicated. If he is mentally retarded, it is possible that he is progressing as well as can be expected for his mental age. One should never assume, however, that speech problems are caused by low mentality until a qualified psychologist has tested the child and given such a verdict. Many children who appear stupid because they do not talk actually have average or above-average intelligence.

C. Speech Models

What sort of speech does the child listen to? Do you, as parents, provide a speech model which is worthy of imitation? He learns to speak by imitating you; perhaps you are remiss in not giving him a good pattern to follow. Do you speak too rapidly? Possibly he has time to hear only parts of the words you say. He may be imitating what he hears, but the speech is so fast that he doesn't catch all of it. Marilyn, a kindergarten child, was a case in point. She was understood only by her mother; she left off the ending of all her words: "A do ca u o da si-wa" meant "A dog came up on the sidewalk." "I wi co da do we I do" was "I will close the door when I go."

D. Experience

Does your child lack a background of experience about which he wants to talk? Most four-year olds are so full of things to say that they can hardly get them out fast enough. In most cases the problem is how to keep them quiet rather than how to get them to talk enough. If your child seems to have nothing to say, you can help by giving him as many varied experiences as you can. Take him to the zoo, on trips and picnics to the beach, to the mountains, and to various parks. Perhaps a television set is essential so that he knows about Mickey Mouse, Howdy Doody, Pinky Lee, Fireman Frank; then he can enter into conversations about them. You can also provide vicarious experience through the story hour, an essential part of every child's home life. Not only is this important for his speech development, but later for his interest in books and in reading. If you have failed to develop his interest in books, you have to be especially careful of your choices at the beginning. Once the habit is established, there will be little trouble and you can depend upon the nightly, "Read me a little story, Daddy."

E. Social Maturity

Speech development is one of the indications of the social maturity of the child. It may be that your child has grown physically, but has not kept pace in his social development. In thinking over this area of conduct, the following questions are useful:

1. Does he walk downstairs one step per tread?
2. Does he dress himself, except for tying?
3. Does he wash his hands and face without assistance?
4. Is he able to care for himself at the toilet?
5. Does he use a pencil or crayon for drawing?
6. Does he feed himself with a spoon and fork?
7. Is he reasonably cautious in protecting himself from danger?
8. Does he cut with scissors?
9. Does he perform for others well enough to be entertaining?
10. Does he help around the house?

If any of these questions is answered in the negative, you may begin to ask yourself why. Has he been given the opportunity to develop these social skills? Have you found it easier to do things for him than to encourage him to do them for himself? You may find that as you get him to "grow up," his speech will improve without your doing anything about it directly. In other words, his speech is merely a reflection of social immaturity; you have solved the problem when you accomplish the matter of getting him to take more responsibility. It is probably no accident that many children with immature speech are the youngest in the family.

F. Home Environment

The happy child is more likely than the unhappy one to develop clear, fluent speech. If your child is having trouble with speech, look for circumstances within the home or the immediate environment which may be causing him concern. Remember, it is not so much the circumstance itself as the way the child feels about it that is important. From your point of view, the item may have little value; from his, it may be the most important factor in his life. From the almost endless possibilities, here are a dozen to start your search:

1. Have you set standards which are too high for him?

Without realizing it, you may have expected more of him than he is ready to achieve. When he failed to live up to your expectations, you let him know that you were disappointed. This setting of standards may have begun with toilet training and continued with eating habits, cleanliness, and company manners. He is aware of the necessity to achieve in order to *please* Mother, or Daddy, or Grandma, or possibly all of you. Because his failures are pointed out rather forcefully, he begins to think of himself as an unworthy individual. He retreats from those situations which call for oral communication. With one child in our clinic this reaction was immediately obvious. Whenever I asked him to do something which he felt he couldn't, he would say that he couldn't or didn't want to. When I urged him he always said, "I'm not talking."

2. Have you compared him unfavorably with other children?

Such comparisons tend to make him feel humiliated and have little or no value in terms of discipline or social development. Each child develops at his own rate and should not be compared to others. Girls usually are at least six months ahead of boys in language development. Accept whatever he is able to do. Give him credit for being as far along as he is in his ability to express himself. Comment on his good qualities and minimize those areas in which he is less adequate.

3. Do you give him time to say what he has to say?

Each child has his own rhythm in doing things. Such reaction time applies also to speech. It is difficult for busy parents to realize that children often take more time than they think is necessary for eating, dressing themselves, and speaking. It will pay in the long run to allow him to progress at his own speed. Some children will say, "Wait a minute. I'm not through yet." Your child may give up his attempt to relate a story and be less inclined to start the next time. Sometimes, in a large family, the less fluent speaker has a hard time getting anything said. Either he fails completely or some other member of the family finishes it for him.

4. Have you been consistent in discipline?

As rule makers for your child, have you agreed upon what he may and may not do? It is confusing for him to be allowed to do something at one time and not allowed to do so another time. Unless, of course, you can make him understand the differing cirumstances. Confusion is compounded when one parent permits certain behavior and the other condemns it. To make matters worse, children become aware that they can play one parent against the other. If grand-parents or other relatives enter into the picture with still other stand-ards, the situation becomes almost hopeless. Confusion over discipline may be reflected in delayed speech, in stuttering, or in both.

The best policy is to agree on a minimum of essential rules and stick to them. Avoid surrounding him by hundreds of "no's." Check up on yourself. Make a list of the times you say "No!" or its equivalent in any one day. Are all of these negations necessary? Maybe you have too many rules. Maybe you are expecting too much of a child of four. Perhaps you could undertake a program of "preventive dis-cipline," that is, provide him with activities that will help to cut down on the necessity for scoldings. Children must have something to do; they can't just sit and be "good."

5. Have you provided a satisfying daily routine for the child?

All children need to have a routine upon which they can depend. Meals must be on time, and at the same time each day. Bedtime should be at a reasonable hour and adhered to, except for rare oc-

Courtesy of Golden Gate Nursery Schools.

Fig. 6. Finger painting provides an outlet for artistic urges.

casions when the child is allowed to stay up. Sufficient sleep and wholesome food are vital to good health—which, in turn, is vital for strong, pleasant, fluent speech.

6. Have you given him avenues of self-expression?

By the time he is four, your child will be wanting to express himself through creative activities. Finger paints, clay, and crayons are avenues to this end. And the product of his endeavor should be taken seriously. The question to be avoided is, "What is that? A house?" Better to say, "Tell me about your drawing, Johnny." If he says that it is a fire truck, then it is.

Some children begin their efforts at creative activity by cutting scraps of paper. Accept this art work. One mother looked at her son's bits of paper of which he was so very proud and remarked, "Throw away that junk. We've got to go now." Let your child feel that you approve of his attempt to express himself. He will develop more recognizable forms of art when he is ready.

Construction toys, such as blocks, tinker toys, or erector sets, help the child to develop skill in creative play. Two or more children can be encouraged to play-act familiar scenes. Simple jig-saw puzzles assist in the recognition of sizes and shapes. Dancing lessons or music instruction provide further possibilities for self-expression.

7. Have you helped him to make friends with other children of his own age?

The lonely child is more likely to have poorly developed speech. Even his brothers and sisters may be too far removed in interests to stimulate his speech activities. Older children may speak for him so that he lacks the necessity to speak for himself. An older sister, with the best intentions of trying to save him embarrassment, may contribute to his poor speech patterns. Younger children may have such poorly developed speech that his speech, by comparison, is "good." If children of his own age are not available in the neighborhood, exchange visits should be arranged with out-of-neighborhood friends or relatives.

Nursery school may be the answer. Some mothers have set up a vicious circle. They don't want to send four-year-old Jimmy to nursery school because he doesn't speak well enough. They are afraid the children at school will make fun of him. Yet, he needs the stimulation of other children to develop his speech. His family can understand him and in his sheltered little world, he manages very well. In a well regulated nursery school he will have opportunities to mature in many ways, in speech, in playing with other children, and in pre-school activities. The child whose speech is immature is more in need of nursery school experience than the child whose speech development is normal.

8. *Have you helped him to develop other skills of which he can be proud?*

Every child needs to feel that he is expert in several activities. He wants to be able to say, "Look at what I can do." The achievement

Courtesy of Golden Gate Nursery Schools.

Fig. 7. Children want to excel at something.

may be catching a ball, playing marbles, drawing a picture, or roller skating. But, all skills must be learned. And, usually, someone must teach them to the child.

If the child has any muscular incoordination, he will need more instruction than other children. You can help him best by joining with him in the games. Teach him by showing him how. The learning process must be fun. The child needs to feel that he can do important things—that he can hold his own with other children his age. This sense of accomplishment will be reflected in improved speech.

9. *Have you added your problems to those of the child?*

Children are especially sensitive to disturbances within the family group. What may appear to you to be a minor problem in finance or in other family relations may loom large in his eyes. He may build it up in his mind until it causes him great anxiety.

Family disputes are often catastrophic to the child. He has no way of knowing that angry words may be soon forgotten. The four-year old wants mother and father to love each other. Any evidence to the contrary is upsetting to him. Some children get upset even when parents tease each other; they take statements at their face value. They cannot understand double meanings, "kidding," or emotionally charged language.

Be careful of your talk before the young child. Save your discussions of troublesome problems until he is out of hearing. Don't depend too much on his being asleep. Children hear bits of conversation through closed doors and then build upon what they hear. In the night, misunderstood or little understood phrases build into bogies which disrupt sleep or lead to nightmares and to hesitancies in speech.

10. *Have you let him know that you accept him, are proud of him, love him?*

It is easy for a child to misinterpret teasing, discipline, or even chance remarks. Unless he is reassured repeatedly, he may get the idea that he is a burden and an unwanted responsibility. Even though he may never mention it, the undercurrent of apprehension may distress him. Just because he does not speak well, he may feel that he has failed to live up to family expectations. He needs reassurance that he is loved and wanted for himself, and that his poor speech and his occasional misbehavior do not alter that basic fact.

This attitude of acceptance must extend to his speech. Although you have not called him lazy, stubborn, or careless, you may have given that impression in indirect ways. You may have said, "Slow down," "Think before you speak," "Take a deep breath," "Susan is only three and she talks better than you do." Reassure him that we all must learn to speak better, that everyone gets mixed up sometimes, that speaking correctly is a difficult job. Any effort which he makes should be accepted; show an interest in what he has to say and encourage him to say more.

11. *Have you allowed your child to express negative feelings as well as positive ones?*

Allow the child to express anti-social feelings. Accept them and help him to interpret them. Rather than, "You mustn't say a thing like that," try, "I know how you feel. You hated Mommy when she put you in your room." Again, "Little sisters can be a nuisance sometimes, can't they?" If you try to suppress the expression of negative feelings, you give him reason for not talking.

Whenever a child feels a need to contradict, or to refuse a request and is not allowed to do so, he is torn between the desire to speak and not to speak. You may remember instances in which similar pressures caused your speech to become broken and tentative. The same result is even more easily reached with the four-year old child. He may not regain his fluency as easily as you do, especially if you call his attention to the fact that he is not speaking well.

12. *Do you treat him as a developing individual personality?*

At four, Johnny is no longer a baby. He must be treated as a big boy. He has a world of his own to which he is entitled. You cannot hold him back or make him conform entirely to your concept of what he should be. Already forces are at work within him to make him a separate individual, not an appendage of his parents, not a younger version of an older brother. His interests, his likes and dislikes must be taken into consideration in making decisions. He is not a puppet to be pushed around; he is an integral part of the family unit. If it is a democratic family, his vote has weight in immediate and long-term planning.

SPEECH TRAINING

For most children of four an indirect approach to speech training is best. They are not ready to deal with individual sounds or to be shown how to make them. However, there are some activities which are helpful in stimulating speech improvement. These are offered to supplement the suggestions given in Chapter I.

A. Conversation

Speak *to* the child, not over him. Use simple language in short sentences. Speak slowly and distinctly so that he hears the speech well. Use the names of things over and over so that he is familiar with them. If he asks for something, repeat the phrase after him without calling attention to the fact that he mispronounced it. For example, he says, "I want a tootie." You say, "A cookie? (stress the "k") Yes, you may have a cookie. What kind of cookie do you want? A brown cookie? Here are the cookies. Which cookie do you want?" Here, you see, you've repeated the word six times. Of course, don't overdo it.

Try to get full sentences in response to questions. Or at least more than "Yeah" or "Nope." You can phrase the questions in such a way that longer answers are required. "Where is the paper?" "What would you like to have for lunch?" or "Where shall we go for a walk?"

B. Scrapbooks

Scrapbooks may be used with some children. Find pictures of things which emphasize the troublesome sounds. In the evening he may show the book to Daddy and name the objects to him. If he is having difficulty with "r," then pictures of "rifle," "train," "radio," "tractor," "radishes," "rabbit," etc. would be helpful. Other pictures may stress the sound in the middle of the word or at the end. Remember, you are interested in the sound—not the name of the letter.

C. Games and Stories

You may play "Follow-The-Leader" with sounds. You produce a sound, such as "fffff" and then ask him to do it. Don't suggest that you are working on speech, but merely "play a game." Use sounds that he can make at first, and then slip in one of the troublesome sounds. Nonsense syllables can be used in the same way, as "boo-boo," "tay-tay," etc. Hide some object and when he gets near it, give a signal, as

Courtesy of Morrison Center for Rehabilitation.

Fig. 8. Scrapbooks can be used for emphasizing sounds. Diane is showing her mother how to say "sh."

"ssss," as a clue that he is "hot." Then he hides the object and you search. He, then, supplies the sound when you get near the hidden object.

You can utilize the story hour to emphasize the poorly articulated sounds. Choose stories in which the sound is emphasized. This tabulated list may get you started:

General Sound Stimulation	Book:	"Noises and Mr. Flibberty-Jib," by Gertrude Crampton
	Record:	"Adventures in Mother Goose Land," RCA Victor—Album Y-34

"p"	Books:	"Pete's Puddle," by Joanna Foster
		"Pretzel," by Margaret Rey
		"Percy, Polly, and Pete," by Clare Turley Newberry
	Record:	"Happy Birthday," by Margaret Wise Brown. Young People's Records. (Years 2-6)
"b"	Books:	"Boku and the Sound," by Lloyd Coe
		"Benny the Bus," by Gladus M. Horn
		"The Big Brown Bear," by Georges Duplaix
		"The Story of Babar," by Jean de Brunhoff
	Record:	"Little Brass Band," Young People's Records. (Years 3-7)

Courtesy of Morrison Center for Rehabilitation.

Fig. 9. Puppets and recording machines stimulate speech.

"m"	Books:	"Madeline," by Ludwig Bemelmans
		"Mike Mulligan and His Steam Shovel," by Virginia Lee Burton
	Record:	"Train to the Zoo," The Children's Record Guild. (CRG-1001) (Years 3-6)

"t"	Books:	"Tiko-Tiko," by Ylla "Tall Enough Tommy," by Becky "Timothy Turtle," by Al Graham "Tootle," by Gertrude Crampton
	Record:	"Playtime Song," Young People's Records. (YPR-1009) (Years 3-6)
"d"	Books:	"Dinny and Danny," by Louis Stobodkin "Who Likes Dinner?" by Evelyn Beyer "Doctor Dan," by Helen Gaspard
	Record:	"Building a City," Young People's Records. (Years 3-7)
"n"	Books:	"Nicodemus," by Inez Hogan "Noodle," by Munro Leaf "Pantaloon," by Kathryn Jackson
	Record:	"Skittery Skattery," The Children's Record Guild. (Years 3-5)
"k"	Books:	"Cowboy Small," by Lois Lenski "The Kittens Who Hid From Their Mother," by Wonder Books, Inc. "The Carrot Seed," by Ruth Krauss
	Record:	"Grandfather's Farm," by the Children's Record Guild. (Years 5-8)
"g"	Books:	"Dr. Goat," by Georgiana "Goat Gruff," Author unknown
	Record:	"The Little Gray Ponies," Young People's Records. (Years 3-6)
"ng"	Books:	"The Story About Ping," by Marjorie Flack and Kurt Weiss "Bongo," by Walt Disney Studios
	Record:	"The Men Who Come to Our House," Young People's Records. (Years 3-6)
"w"	Books:	"The Wet World," by Norma Simon "Willie Goes to the Seashore," by Pauline Vinson
	Record:	"Mary Doodle," The Children's Record Guild. (Years 3-6)
"f"	Books:	"Fast Is Not a Ladybug," by Miriam Schlein "Fun with Animal Faces," by Julian Wehr "The Little Fire Engine," by Lois Lenski
	Record:	"Happy Birthday," by Margaret Wise Brown. Young People's Records. (Years 2-6)

"th"	Books:	"Jonathan," by Sally Scott "The Three Little Horses," Piet Werm
	Record:	"Mary Doodle," The Children's Record Guild. (Years 3-6)
"h"	Books:	"Heavy Is a Hippopotamus," by Miriam Schlein
	Record:	"First Music for Ones and Twos," The Children's Record Guild. (Years 2-4)
"l"	Books:	"Ola," by Ingie and Edgar D'Aulaire "The Sleepy Little Lion," by Ylla "Plink Plink," by Ethel and Leonard Kessler
	Record:	"Out of Doors," Young People's Records. (Years 2-6)
"r"	Books:	"Little Bruin and Par," by Haskin Christensen "One Morning in Maine," by Robert McCloskey
	Record:	"Sunday in the Park," by The Children's Record Guild.
"s"	Books:	"Little Black Sambo," by Helen Bannerman "So'm I," by Ted Key "Socks," by Betty Molgard Ryan "Let's Find Skipper," by Jeffrey Victor
	Record:	"Out of Doors," Young People's Records. (Years 2-6)
"z"	Books:	"Tiger Tizzy," by Joseph Longstreet "Zic-Zac," by Rita Kissin
	Record:	"Bozo on the Farm," Capitol Records. (Years 3-6)
"sh"	Books:	"The Brave Little Steam Shovel," by Alf Evers "Little Shepherd," by Annabell Armour
	Record:	"The Carrot Seed," by The Children's Record Guild. (Years 3-6)
"j"	Books:	"Curious George Takes A Job," by H. A. Rey "Journey Cake-Ho," by Ruth Sawyer "Bear Twins," by Inez Hogan
	Record:	"Johnny Appleseed," RCA Victor. (Years 5-8)

| "ch" | Books: | "Chicken Little," by M. A. Donohue and Co. "Chip-Chip," by Little Golden Books "Ching-Li," by Martha Lee Poston |
| | Record: | "Train to the Farm," The Children's Record Guild. (Years 3-6) |

SUMMARY STATEMENT

By the time the child is four, he should have intelligible speech. He may still have two or more faulty sounds, but he should be able to express himself in full sentences. If he does not, he needs help. Someone outside the home, preferably a speech correctionist, might be asked to help. You can do a great deal in the home by trying to find the causes of his speech difficulties, and removing or minimizing these causal factors. Direct work with speech at this age is difficult, but many indirect techniques may be employed to stimulate better speech production. Don't sit back with the attitude that "He will grow out of it."

BOOKS TO READ

ANDERSON, VIRGIL A.: *Improving the Child's Speech.* New York, Oxford University Press, 1953.

BACKUS, OLLIE, AND BEASLEY, JANE: *Speech Therapy with Children.* New York, Houghton Mifflin Company, 1951.

BARUCH, DOROTHY: *New Ways in Discipline.* New York, McGraw-Hill Book Company, 1949.

ILG, FRANCES, AND AMES, LOUISE BATES: *Child Behavior.* New York, Harper and Brothers, 1955.

KAWIN, ETHEL: *The Wise Choice of Toys.* Chicago, University of Chicago Press, 1938.

KELLOGG, RHODA: *Babies Need Fathers, Too.* New York, Comet Press Books, 1953.

CHAPTER III

CORRECTING FAULTY SPEECH

To: Adults who are helping others to overcome speech defects

Y our child is ten years old, but his speech is obviously not adequate for his age. He resents the teasing of his classmates.

You have been unable to obtain professional speech therapy. Your son needs help with his speech. Therefore, you are determined to help him yourself.

You must understand, at the outset, that it is extremely difficult for a parent to give speech instruction. Even though you know what to do, the child may resent your efforts. So often mothers report, "But Bobby won't let me help him. If I mention his speech, he just gets mad." Unless you can win the child over to the idea of working directly on his speech, you had better stick to the indirect method suggested in Chapters I and II.

We are assuming that your speech is free from obvious errors. You are able to provide him with a correct model as you bombard him with the sound upon which you are concentrating. Furthermore, you have the patience to work painstakingly with a child who finds it difficult to change speech habits of several years' standing. Even though you have not had special training in speech or in teaching, you are willing to make the effort to study the child's speech problems so that, together, you can attack them systematically. Granted that these prerequisites are fulfilled, you are ready to begin.

EXAMINING HIS SPEECH

A starting point is to determine what is wrong with the child's speech. Ask him to read the following sentences. Notice only the sound which is being stressed in each sentence. Take notes so that you are able to make a summary of the incorrect sounds. He may omit a sound, as "tee" for "tree" or "nake" for "snake." He may substitute one sound for another, as "fum" for "thumb" or "dun" for "gun." He may add a sound, as "goingk" for "going." He may produce the correct sound, but does so in a faulty manner, such as a "slushy s" or a "snorted ch."

1. .... ä .... His father started the car.
2. .... ō .... Go inside and open the window.
3. .... ŭ .... The cup was made of rubber.
4. .... ă .... The man ran after his hat.
5. .... ē .... Each person should eat some meat.
6. .... ĭ .... William threw his mit at the kitten.
7. .... ā .... She is baking a cake today.
8. .... ĕ .... The pet robin got wet in her nest.
9. .... ōō .... You may have two of the blue books.
10. .... ŏŏ .... Dan took a good look at the crook.
11. .... ô .... The eagle caught the small bird in his claw.
12. .... ī .... The kite flew high in the sky.
13. .... ou .... The mouse ran out of the house.
14. .... oi .... The boy made a noise with the toy.
15. .... p .... Put the apples on the ship.
16. .... b .... Bob kept the rabbit in a tub.
17. .... m .... Mary paid a dime for the hammer.
18. .... t .... Betty would not take off her coat.
19. .... d .... Did you buy some candy today?
20. .... n .... Nobody can tell a funny story.
21. .... k .... Can you wait a second for some milk?
22. .... g .... Sugar is not good on an egg.
23. .... ng .... A new bank is going to open in the Spring.
24. .... w .... We will walk between the houses.
25. .... hw (wh) .... Where did the bobwhite go?
26. .... h .... He said, "Hello," in a happy voice.
27. .... th .... I think I will take a bath on Thursday.
28. .... th .... That man is my father.
29. .... f .... He made coffee after five o'clock.
30. .... v .... They gave her the stove as a valentine present.
31. .... sh .... She knows the ocean is full of fish.

32. .... zh .... It was a pleasure to measure the room.
33. .... y .... Yes, I ate the onion yesterday.
34. .... ch .... The teacher put her watch on the chair.
35. .... j .... The pigeon will jump out of the cage.
36. .... s .... Susan read her lesson for the class.
37. .... z .... The busy bee was buzzing near the barn.
38. .... l .... Twelve people were out on the lake.
39. .... r .... The room was full of rabbits.
40. .... er .... Does the early bird get the worm?

For children who are unable to read, pictures of objects may be used to elicit desired sounds.

As the child talks you will want to notice his voice (or tone) as well as the articulation of the individual sounds. These questions will help you to complete your evaluation:

1. Is the speech too fast or too slow?
2. Is the pitch too high or too low?
3. Is the voice too loud or too soft?
4. Is the voice unpleasant to hear?
   a. Is it harsh?
   b. Is it hoarse?
   c. Is it nasal?
   d. Is it breathy?

Now you are ready to summarize your findings. Typical summary statements might be:

"Bobby mumbles; his voice is nasal; he substitutes "w" for "r"; and he omits "s" when it occurs with another consonant, as "st," "sm," or "sk."

"Bobby cannot be heard across the room; his voice is breathy; he substitutes "f" for "th," and he has a poor "s."

REMOVING THE CAUSAL FACTORS

Now you know specifically what is wrong with your child's speech. The next step is to search for any factors which may be causing the difficulty. Usually, a number of factors combine to cause speech which varies from the normal pattern. You should investigate as many potential factors as possible and try to eliminate them. We may assume that you have looked for the environmental factors described in Chapter II, and that you have made what changes you can in conditions which affect his speech.

The child's hearing should be checked with an audiometer. If there is considerable loss, he may need to use a hearing aid; in addition, lip reading instruction may be necessary. Sounds must be amplified so that he can hear them as other people hear them. Once he is aware of the correct sound, he may be able to reproduce it.

Children who are low in mentality need more stimulation than the average child to produce intelligible speech. Although many persons with speech defects have normal or even superior intelligence, generally speaking, mental ability and language facility are closely related. Once a psychologist has determined that a child is mentally deficient, special training should be provided to develop his language to its fullest extent. Speech therapy, begun at an early age and continued over many years, may give him oral communication skills which would otherwise be impossible.

The way in which the upper and lower teeth fit together is very important for correct speech. Although the closing (occlusion) need not be perfect, it must be reasonably good. If some of the teeth are missing or if the upper front teeth protrude too far, it is very difficult to make the "s," "z," "sh," and "ch" sounds satisfactorily. Sometimes

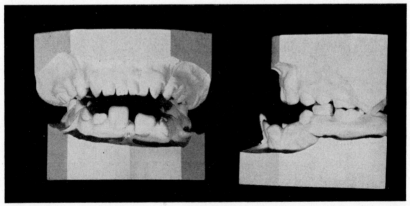

Courtesy of Wendell Wylie, M.D., San Francisco.

Fig. 10. Orthodontia may be necessary before speech therapy can be effective.

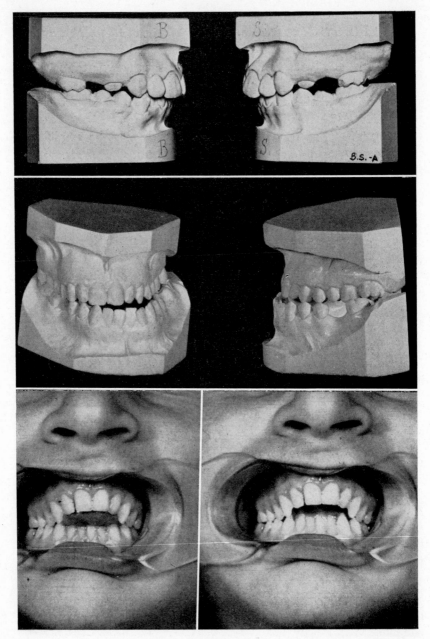

Fig. 11
Overbite.
Underbite.
Openbite.

the lower front teeth protrude beyond the upper teeth; in other cases the upper and lower front teeth do not meet and there is an open-bite. When any of these conditions exists, it is possible for the tongue to make adjustments to stop the air stream and direct it through the proper channel. But the tongue can do only so much; orthodontia (teeth straightening) may be necessary before normal speech can be produced.

Courtesy of School for Cerebral Palsied Children, Northern California.

Fig. 12. Healthy children have more energy to apply to the job of learning to speak.

The general health of the child is important to his speech and language development. Perhaps he is often too tired to make the necessary effort for correct speech. The solution to the speech problem starts with better food, regular hours of rest, and plenty of outdoor exercise. Or possibly general muscular coordination is poor, that is, the child is clumsy and moves in an awkward manner. Here again, speech is only one aspect of a more general physical condition. In some cases, dancing lessons, skating lessons and the like may be an essential part of the speech improvement program. Sound deviations and poor voice quality may clear up as he feels more confident of himself—more equal to life's demands.

IMPROVING SPEECH

In speech work, it is helpful to use a recording machine. Then you can hear any imperfections more easily. Your recorded speech may sound somewhat different to you because you are hearing it through your ear alone. Previously, you have heard your speech through the bones of your head as well as your ear. You may be hearing it for the first time as other people hear it. Your speech may be better, or possibly worse, than you thought.

A. Breath Control

The production of tone for speech depends upon the control of the exhaled breath stream. As the air is pushed out of the lungs up through the wind pipe, it is forced between the vocal folds, or cords, in the voice box. These cords must vibrate easily and freely in order to produce a clear, strong tone.

Have the "patient" say "ah" in a relaxed manner. Can he hold a clear unwavering tone for the count of ten? Is the tone loud enough to be heard across the room? Try other vowels, as "ā," "ē," and "ō."

Courtesy of Morrison Center for Rehabilitation.

Fig. 13. Blowing out a candle is a step toward breath control for speech.

If these tones are weak, he needs to breathe more deeply. To encourage him to build up the air supply, use a count of three.

Breathe in: one—two—three

To breathe out, or exhale, he should contract the abdominal muscles. This action squeezes the air out of the lungs, up through the voice box, and on into the throat. From here it escapes through the mouth or the nose depending on whether the gateway between the mouth and the nose is open or closed. As soon as he establishes the correct breathing pattern, he can start tone on the outgoing breath stream.

Breathe in: one—two—three.

Breathe out: Say "ah." (Hold for a count of ten.)

At first he may not be able to hold the tone long enough. Each practice period, try for a little more tone until ten is reached. That much elongation will be sufficient for ordinary conversation. Only three sounds, "m," "n," and "ng," are emitted through the nose; so be sure that all vowel sounds are emitted through the mouth.

B. Relaxation

It is necessary that he be relaxed as he is producing these tones. Any tenseness in the speech equipment will contribute to harsh, high-pitched tones. It is advisable to precede each practice period with a few minutes of relaxation. Have him sit in an easy chair or lie down and collapse completely. Yawning is good for relaxation of the throat muscles. For speech to be correct, it must be produced in an easy, effortless manner.

Any factors in the environment which add to the child's nervousness should be carefully checked. Maybe he is being overstimulated by too many activities. One father reported in our clinic, "I don't know what makes Joey nervous. But we do yell at him a lot." In this case, a change in method of discipline was a key factor in Joey's improved speech. An earlier bedtime may be advisable. These few suggestions may start you on an investigation of tension-producing factors in your child's daily routine.

C. Eliminating Breathy Tone

Breathiness of tone results when the vocal cords do not come together properly. Too much air escapes between them and gives the speech a "whispered" quality. Provided there is nothing physically wrong with the voice box—an examination by a laryngologist is needed to determine this—the following procedure usually clears up the trouble. Practice a sharp attack on the vowels. This is just the opposite of the procedure recommended for work on harshness, hoarseness, or nasality. Force the air out of the lungs quickly and bring the vocal cords together with a "bang." Imagine a drill master before a squadron of soldiers barking out commands: "ā," "ē," "ī," "ō," "ōō."

D. Avoiding Nasality

Tone is produced in the voice box and then is transmitted to the mouth. Here, the shaping of the vowels and consonants takes place by the action of the articulatory equipment: the palate, tongue, teeth, lips, and jaw.

The palate (roof of the mouth) divides the mouth cavity from the nasal (nose) cavity; the back part, the soft palate, must move up to close the gateway between the throat and nose. When it fails to do so, air escapes through the nose and we find the resulting speech unpleasant because of its nasality. Of course, the soft palate must move downward to allow the sounds "m," "n," and "ng" to go through the nose. The movement of this muscle can be checked: Have the child open his mouth wide and say alternately, "ah"—"ng." The easiest method for knowing when to raise and lower the soft palate is listening. That is, the child must learn to hear the difference between the acceptable tone and the nasal tone.

In some parts of the country nasality is not considered unpleasant, but in others it is distasteful. To overcome nasality, three procedures are recommended:

1. Open the mouth wider than usual so that the sound can escape and will not be forced through the nose. Many people who have nasal voices speak with clenched teeth. Simply speak with freer jaw action; shape the vowels more carefully, using the lips and tongue more precisely.

2. Speak in a more relaxed manner. As the muscles of the mouth and throat relax, nasality tends to disappear.

3. Train the ear to hear the difference between speech which is nasal and that which is acceptable. Pinch the nose shut with your fingers to eliminate any vibration in the nose during speech. Then say a phrase or sentence in which there are no "m," "n," or "ng"

sounds since the nose must not be blocked to make these sounds. After you have spoken the phrase or sentence with the nose pinched closed, repeat without pinching the nose to determine if there is any difference in the two performances.

Samples sentences:
a. I bought a black hat.
b. Joe asked Alice to go to the show.
c. Father waited at the store.
d. Charlie sold his car yesterday.
e. Lois was late for school today.

E. Shaping the Vowels

People who talk with the teeth clenched together fail to open the mouth enough to allow the sounds to get out. When the sounds cannot go through the mouth as they should, they are pushed up through the nose and thus contribute to a nasal quality which is unpleasant. For practice exaggerate the opening of the mouth. It is unlikely that this unnatural manner of forming the vowels will carry over into conversation. If it does, a reminder of the difference between practice and "real" speech will help out.

If the lips are lazy or sluggish, practice on "ee"–"oo." Start the two sounds slowly, saying each one distinctly. Gradually increase the speed; watch in a mirror to be sure that the lips are drawn back sharply and then rounded tightly. Further practice should include the "ah" position, thus: "ee–ah–oo." Special emphasis upon opening the mouth wide develops an awareness of jaw movement. "Yah, yah, yah" can be said slowly and then speeded up. Flexibility of the jaw and lips is essential to good speech.

The tongue is very important in articulating sounds. Any sluggishness in its movement will make the speech sounds muffled and unclear. In rare cases, there is tongue tie. If it should occur, a physician can cut the tissue under the tongue to free it for full movement. These tongue exercises are helpful in activating a sluggish tongue:
1. Stick your tongue out as far as you can.
2. Try to touch the tip of your nose.
3. Push your tongue out and in as fast as you can.
4. Try to touch your chin with your tongue.
5. Lick your lips with your tongue.

6. Move your tongue from side to side, increasing in speed.

7. Sweep the roof of your mouth with your tongue.

8. With your mouth open say "la-la-la," first very slowly and then faster.

Careful shaping of the vowels is vital to clear and melodious speech. The following groups are given for special practice:

Group I

Draw the lips back in a smiling position; open the mouth slightly.

	beginning	*middle*	*ending*
ē:	each	bean	knee
	eat	meat	sea
	even	teeth	tree
ĭ:	inch	mit	
	Indian	tin	
	itch	vim	

Group II

Open the mouth wide; produce a relaxed tone.

ă:	add	battle
	apple	fast
	ax	traffic
ä:	arm	car
	argue	farm
	arson	marble

Group III

Round the lips into a circle; make the circle smaller for the second vowel group.

ō:	open	home	go
	over	cold	low
	own	soap	throw
ōō:	ooze	boot	blue
		moon	shoe
		soon	true

Group IV

Diphthongs combine two vowels into one sound. They start with the first vowel and then quickly slide into the second.

au: ä - ōo

ouch	brown	cow
out	mouse	now
owl	town	plow

ī: ä - ĭ

ice	like	die
idea	time	pie
iron	wise	spy

If the chief difficulty is in volume, pitch, or quality—then you will need to emphasize relaxation, correct breathing, and the proper formation of vowels. The first fifteen lessons in the Appendix provide additional drills on the vowels and diphthongs.

F. Working on the Consonants

The child's speech is loud enough for you to hear; the quality is pleasing; the pitch is satisfactory—but you have difficulty in understanding him. You have found in your examination of his speech that certain consonants are incorrectly produced. Your notes indicate which sounds are being substituted for other sounds, which are omitted, and which are distorted. Material for each consonant is given in Lessons 17-40 in the Appendix, but some advice on procedure is necessary.

You are not an expert in speech therapy, nor do you intend to become one. But it would be helpful for you to understand how the consonants are interrelated. They are the beginnings and endings of the vowels, which form the base of the syllable. If that beginning is just breath without any tone, or voice, it is a whispered consonant, such as "h" or "p." When there is tone, the consonant is voiced, as "d" or "z."

Consonants may be divided into groups according to the manner in which they are formed. Six consonants are called *plosives* because the outgoing air stream is stopped by the lips or the tongue and then allowed to burst forth suddenly.

Voiced	*Whispered*
b (boy)	p (pie)
d (dog)	t (toe)
g (go)	k (king)

The *fricatives* are made when air is forced over a surface, such as the lips, teeth, or tongue. This friction noise is essential to the sound.

Voiced	*Whispered*
v (vine)	f (five)
th (these)	th (thing)
z (zero)	s (see)
zh (measure)	sh (shoe)
	h (hoe)

Two consonants are a combination of a plosive and a fricative. "T" and "sh" blend together to make "ch," as in "China"; while "d" and "zh" combine to form "j," as in "Joe." "Ch" is a whispered sound; "j" is voiced.

"M," "n," and "ng" are called *nasals* because they are emitted through the nose. Only these three sounds in English are sent through the nose; all others should be expelled through the mouth.

Some consonants are very similar to vowels and are often difficult for young children to produce. The ear must be trained very carefully to make these particular consonants, known as *semi-vowels*.

w (water)

l (look)

r (rose)

y (yes)

There is usually not much difficulty with "w," but it may be substituted for any or all of the others in this group.

One other sound combination is that of "h" and "w" (wh). Actually the "h" is said first and the "w" follows. For correct speech this sound is needed for such words as "when," "what," and "whistle," but it is not essential to understanding. To use "w" instead of "hw" produces careless speech, not defective speech.

The basis for correction is ear training. You must teach the child to recognize the sound which you want him to accept into his speech. Then you can teach him how to make the correct sound and how to use the new sound in combination with various vowels. Lastly, help him to carry over this new sound into his speech. At first the carry-over will be with a few selected words; then it will spread to his conversational speech. Follow these steps for each sound you wish to change. (The order in which the new sounds should be taught is suggested by the arrangement of the practice lessons in the Appendix.)

Step I: The Sound by Itself

Let's suppose that Bobby has a lisp, that is, he substitutes "th" for "s." He says "thaw" for "saw," "bithycle" for "bicycle," and "buth" for "bus." You can introduce him to the "snake" sound as a separate "noise," apart from speech. He must learn to identify the sound when you produce it. You can make various sounds—as "t-t-t-t," "er-er-er," "ch-ch-ch," and "s-s-s-s-." He may sit with his right hand in a fist. When he hears the "snake" sound, he lifts his index finger. You can hide a penny and have him look for it. When he is near, you make the "snake" sound as a signal.

Courtesy of Morrison Center for Rehabilitation.

Fig. 14. The "snake sound" is fun to learn.

When he has learned to identify the snake sound, you ask him to produce it. You can say, "I will make the sound three times and you make it once."

Visual cues are very important in making many of the consonants, especially "s" and "z.". You say, "Watch me as I make the sound. Notice that I keep my front teeth together and my tongue is hidden." You may sit beside him before a mirror. Ask him to watch you as you make the sound and then to watch himself. "Make it just as I do." Explain that the breath must come out between the middle front teeth. If he still is unable to produce the correct sound, ask him to start with the "t" position and continue with "s." He may even say "ts" at first.

It often takes several lessons, one-half hour each time, before the child is able to produce the sound. Meantime, you can use a variety of ways to bombard his ear with the correct sound. Use sentences which contain one or more snake sounds and ask him to indicate when the snake sound occurs. Exaggerate the production of the sound slightly for his benefit.

1. The girl was carrying a silk umbrella.
2. You may borrow my pencil for a minute.
3. We should take the bus into the country.
4. The sun did not go down until eight o'clock.
5. He did not see the man who walked away.

Without calling particular attention to the sound, read stories which have it in prominent positions, as the name of the main character in "Little Black Sambo."

Step II: The Sound in Nonsense Syllables

Before too long, progress to nonsense syllables. It is frustrating both to you and to the child to spend too much time on the first step. Each lesson period you can review the sound in isolation. Combine the "s" with vowels

sā	sē	sī	sō	sōo
ās	ēs	īs	ōs	ōos
āsā	ēsē	īsī	ōsō	ōosōo

His first successful production of the sound may be in the middle between two vowels or at the end of the nonsense syllable.

You can continue ear training by asking him which of the words you pronounce begin with the snake sound: rabbit, milk, *scissors*, ladder. And you will want to slip in a word beginning with the sound (th) which he has been using in place of the snake sound, as: paper, thing, *song*, turtle. You can show him a page with two columns of words. Ask him to point to the one of the pair which you say.

thing	sing
thought	sought
thank	sank
thick	sick
thin	sin

Step III: *The Sound in Words* ....

When the child is able to make the sound in nonsense (play) syllables, proceed to "real" words. It will probably be easier for him to put the "snake" sound in new words than in ones he has been saying incorrectly for several years.

Beginning	Middle	End
said	lesson	mouse
soft	blessing	horse
sing	lassie	rice
safe	baseball	race
sail	missing	yes

Step IV: *The Sound in Blend Words*

The next step is to practice some of the more difficult blends, that is, "s" with another consonant.

smart	master	hats
sneeze	whisper	cooks
speak	asleep	traps
star	basket	depths
skate	upset	tenths
swing	understand	beast
sleep	restring	wrist
splice	sightseeing	nests
straw	statistics	vests

Step V: The Sound in Sentences

Typical sentences for practice are given in Lesson 36 in the Appendix.

Step VI: Transfering to Connected Speech

The final phase of speech re-education is transferring the new sound into conversation. It is impossible for the child to be careful all the time. Special periods should be set aside as "good speech" time. During this period, perhaps half an hour each day, the family may call his attention to errors in using the new sound. The special period might be the dinner hour, or the time while he is helping with cleaning up. Whenever it is, he should agree to it. As he improves, the periods of carefulness are increased until finally he is corrected whenever he forgets.

One technique to use when he is well along the road to using the sound—though he still makes occasional slips—is for you to make an error to see if he will catch it. For example, you say, "Bobby, what did you do at thkool today?" If he doesn't notice it, just continue without drawing it to his attention. He will probably say, "What was that?" or "No, not 'thkool' but 'school.'"

This rather extended discussion of correcting a central lisp was used as an illustration. You would follow the same general steps in correcting any individual sound. Modifications need to be made according to the sound and the reasons it is not being made correctly. Within the lessons in the Appendix suggestions are given concerning the teaching of each of the sounds.

SPECIAL PROBLEMS

Defective speech may be much more involved and complicated than the substitution of "t" for "k" or the distortion of an "s." The services of a speech therapist are needed. Unfortunately, because of the expense and/or the availability of the therapist, the major portion of the speech correction falls upon the untrained person.

Some suggestions about three rather common types of speech problems are given in the following pages.

A. Foreign Accent

English is one of the most difficult languages in the world. When the young child is surrounded by English all the time, the absorption is gradual and painless. But when he must learn English as a second language, his problems are many and complex. Suppose, for example, that Pedro at age five is sent to school. He has never spoken English and he knows only a few words. Because Spanish is spoken at home, he must maintain his Spanish and at the same time learn a new language.

Pedro has little desire to learn English. His family speaks Spanish and so do his friends. He is a timid little boy and just going to school is frightening enough without the added burden of language. Since he does his thinking in Spanish, he must translate everything into Spanish equivalents before he can retain it. So the building up of an oral vocabulary becomes a first task. Because two words, Spanish

Courtesy of Golden Gate Nursery Schools.

Fig. 15. Drum beats can catch the rhythm of English.

and English, must be learned for most things, the process is slow and requires much repetition. Some English words are similar to those in Spanish, but most words are not exactly the same either in spelling or pronunciation.

Word order and grammar are more difficult in English than in many other languages. So also is the melody pattern. Foreign speaking individuals must learn the inflections of English. The most noticeable inflections occur at the ends of sentences. The ordinary declarative sentence ends with a downward inflection:

I saw you last night.

I ran down the street.

Questions end in either an upward or a downward inflection depending on how they are worded. Questions which can be answered with "Yes" or "No" end with an upward inflection.

Shall we go?

Did you close the door?

Questions which begin with a pronoun or adverb (interrogative) and require other than "Yes" or "No" end with a downward inflection.

Why did he go?

Who took my paper?

Where did the dog bite you?

When will we get going?

In addition to the problems of language, vocabulary, and sentence structure (including melody), there is also the matter of pronunciation. English has some sounds, such as "ă" (cat), which are not found in the Romance languages. It does not have others, such as some of the guttural sounds in the German language. The suggestions given in this chapter and in the lessons in the Appendix are guides in overcoming difficulties in pronunciation.

B. Cleft Palate

Cleft palate is a faulty fusion of the two halves of the roof of the mouth before birth. When the child is born, there is a hole in the hard palate (front) or a split in the soft palate (back), or both. There may also be a cleft lip. Sometimes there is a cleft lip with no damage to the palate. The cause of cleft palate is unknown. With modern surgery and orthodontia, most cleft palate children will have adequate repair so that they can develop normal speech.

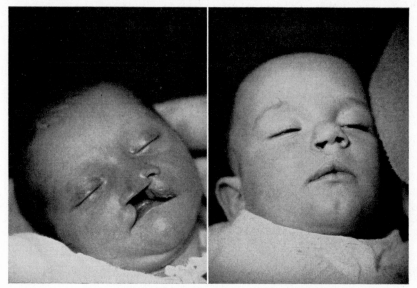

Courtesy of George Warren Pierce, M.D. and Horace Klabunde, M.D.

Fig. 16. Cleft lip before surgery.   Fig. 17. The same cleft lip after surgery.

These children will need more help and encouragement to develop speech than the average child. Because of their susceptibility to colds, they often develop middle ear infections which result in hearing loss. They must be hospitalized for their operations and may be denied normal speech stimulation at home and on the playground. Until adequate repair has been made, they are unable to speak well enough to make themselves understood. Some children retreat from speech situations. As a result of these conditions, the cleft palate child may learn to speak later than the child with a normal palate.

The family can do much to aid the cleft palate child in developing speech. He should be treated as any other child in terms of discipline and home responsibilities. The fact that his palate is different needs to be minimized. Cleft palate cases are among the most hopeful of speech-handicapped children. Most of them can learn to speak normally, frequently before they start to school.

Formal speech training, under the guidance of a qualified speech therapist, should begin at the age of three. Even before that the parents should receive instruction about stimulating speech and language development. Allowing the child to reach school age before speech therapy begins is a waste of at least two precious years when the speech might be completely corrected. In some cases, because of the severity of the cleft, insufficient length of the palate, loss of hearing, or other complicating factors, the child's speech is not perfect even after a year or more of training in speech. Usually, it is greatly improved and his speech is intelligible. Further improvement may depend upon additional surgery, orthodontia, or social maturity.

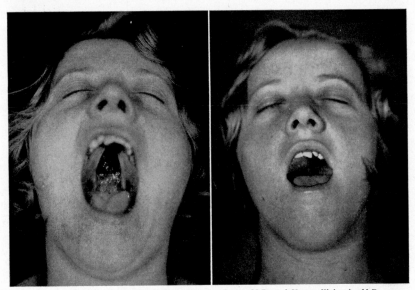

Courtesy of George Warren Pierce, M.D. and Horace Klabunde, M.D.

Fig. 18. Cleft Palate in an adult before surgery.

Fig. 19. The same cleft palate after surgery. Usually the operation is performed when the individual is very young.

A basic problem in cleft palate speech is to teach the child to emit his breath through the mouth instead of the nose. Blowing exercises can be utilized, such as blowing out candles, blowing pinwheels, or blowing a ping-pong ball across a table. Care must be taken not to over-emphasize the emission of air through the mouth. Such over-emphasis causes snorting sounds and a distortion of the consonants. Closure of the passageway between the back of the mouth and the nose can be encouraged by practice on the sounds "ah" - "ng" in rapid succession. For "ah" the soft palate moves upward to close the gateway; for "ng" it moves downward in order to allow the breath stream to go through the nose.

There is usually need for special drill on several of the consonant sounds, especially the plosives and the fricatives (see classification of sounds on page 43). A re-learning of tongue position is often necessary; the cleft palate child may have established incorrect tongue positions in his attempts to compensate for insufficient movement of the palate. Suggestions for teaching correct placement of the tongue and lips are given in the lessons in the Appendix.

C. Cerebral Palsy

Cerebral palsy results from an injury to the central nervous system either before, during, or after birth. The functioning of some muscles, possibly including those used for speech, is imperfect. Speech therapy should be included as a part of the general program, which consists of physical and occupational therapy as well as academic training. From one-half to two-thirds of cerebral palsied individuals have speech deviations from the normal pattern. Breathing exercises, as well as drills for flexibility of the various articulatory muscles—lips, tongue, jaw, and palate—are a vital part of the schedule.

Training in sound discrimination—ear training—is basic to speech therapy for the cerebral palsied. If the child is also hard of hearing, amplification of the speech sounds may be necessary. The speech training program is likely to be a long and arduous one. In severe cases it must be continued for years; even then the speech may remain indistinct and difficult to understand. Relaxation, too, both on the part of the therapist and of the patient is essential. Oftentimes, the harder the patient tries to speak correctly, the more tense he becomes and instead of making his speech better, he makes it worse. "Try easy" is a good motto for the speech efforts of the cerebral palsied.

Slowness of rate and a tendency to use voice (or tone) on the whispered sounds are typical problems of the cerebral palsied. They may run words together and continue the tone instead of stopping one word or phrase and then beginning another. These errors should be brought to their attention. Until they are conscious of what they are doing wrong, they have little chance to make corrections. As they become, through ear training, more aware of their speech sounds, they begin to detect the errors and make efforts to correct them.

There are eight pairs of consonants with which the cerebral palsied individual must be especially careful. He is likely to use voice with the whispered member of the pair and thus distort his pronunciation. He must turn off the "motor" for the whispered sound.

Whispered Sound	Voiced Sound
1. "p"	"b"
pie	buy
apple	cable
cap	cab
2. "t"	"d"
tie	die
latter	ladder
mat	mad
3. "k"	"g"
coat	goat
backing	bagging
tack	tag
4. "th"	"th"
thin	then
ether	either
bath	bathe
5. "f"	"v"
fine	vine
often	oven
half	have
6. "s"	"z"
soon	zoom
mister	miser
cross	craws
7. "sh"	"zh"
shoe	azure
machine	measure
rush	rouge
8. "ch"	"j"
chump	jump
teacher	soldier
rich	ridge

Additional material for each of the voiced and whispered sounds is given in the Appendix.

Courtesy of Morrison Center for Rehabilitation.

Fig. 20. Audio-visual aids, such as records and pictures may give emphasis to word and sound building.

Another error which cerebral palsied persons often make is putting a slight vowel sound between the two consonants in a blend. These two or three initial consonant sounds in a syllable should be made as a single unit. For example:

Incorrect Form	*Correct Form*
buread	bread
gulass	glass
gureen	green
buright	bright
bulue	blue
thuree	three
pulease	please
puroud	proud

Any activities which improve the general muscular coordination of the cerebral palsied individal may be reflected in improved speech. This is especially true when breathing, jaw movement, or flexibility of the tongue becomes more nearly adequate. Tone production problems can be handled much as they would be for other persons. These procedures are described earlier in this chapter. Other suggestions for improvement of language development are given in Chapters I and II.

SUMMARY

An indirect approach to problems in voice production and articulation is not adequate with older children and adults. Someone needs to help them change faulty habits which have made their speech defective. This friend must have good speech which can be used as a model by the speech-handicapped child or adult. He must also be able to listen carefully to determine just what sounds are incorrectly produced. Then, in a systematic fashion, he must attack each aspect of the speech problem and set up exercises which will benefit his "patient."

Actual speech exercises should be preceded, especially in voice problems, by a medical examination to make sure that practice will not be harmful. Whenever possible, the therapy should be supervised by a qualified speech therapist. Much can be done, however, to improve speech even if a therapist is not available. Too often, instead of growing out of a speech defect, the unaided speech-handicapped person merely sets the faulty habits more firmly. The suggestions presented in this chapter, if faithfully followed, will lead the patient toward normal speech.

BOOKS TO READ

ANDERSON, VIRGIL A.: *Improving the Child's Speech*. New York, Oxford University Press, 1953.

JOHNSON, WENDELL, et al.: *Speech Handicapped School Children*. New York, Harper and Brothers, 1948.

MYKELBUST, HELMER: *Your Deaf Child*. Springfield, Ill., Charles C Thomas, Publisher, 1950.

NEMOY, ELIZABETH, AND DAVIS, SERENA: *The Correction of Defective Consonant Sounds*. Boston, Expression Company, 1937.

RUTHERFORD, BERNEICE R.: *Give Them a Chance to Talk*. Minneapolis, Minn., Burgess Publishing Co., 1950.

SCOTT, LOUISE BINDER, AND THOMPSON, J. J.: *Talking Time*. St. Louis, Webster Publishing Company, 1951.

VAN RIPER, CHARLES: *Speech Correction: Principles and Methods*. New York, Prentice-Hall, Inc., 1944.

CHAPTER IV

STUTTERING

To: One who stutters (and/or to the parents of those
who stutter)

In the United States more than a million persons stutter or have stuttered at one time. You, as one of them, have found stuttering to be a baffling and sometimes maddening aspect of living. "Why should I have this affliction?" you ask. "Why can't I speak fluently?"

Professional speech therapists in all parts of the United States have been studying the problem of the non-fluent speaker. They have found data which will be of interest to you. General agreement is that stuttering is not physical in nature; there is nothing wrong with the functioning of the lungs, vocal cords, or muscles of articulation. The tongue, for example, works perfectly well for chewing food and for swallowing. It is only when speech is involved that it seems to "act up," or get "stuck." As long ago as 1894, Dr. Leopold Treitel, a German physician, called stuttering a nervous disorder. Today various terms are used, such as "semantic," "psychic," or "emotional," but they all add up to the conclusion that stuttering is the result of the attitude of the speaker toward the speaking situation.

We know that there is no ready cure, no panacea for stuttering. Schools have been set up which guarantee cures in a few weeks, but, unfortunately, most of the participants have failed to receive permanent benefits. Overcoming your stuttering is likely to be a long and very gradual process. Most authorities agree that the adult stutterer will always stutter, at least at times. You may, however, learn to control the repetitions or hesitations so well that your non-fluency will be unobserved—except on "bad days."

Certain other data have been collected by the research departments of university speech clinics. There is a tendency for stuttering to run in families. The question remains, however, whether stuttering is inherited. More likely, the environment provided by such families

57

affects various members of the family. A mother is more watchful of speech production in her young son if Uncle Jack or Cousin Bess is a stutterer. She is more inclined to interpret the normal hesitancies and sputterings of the young child as undesirable.

At one time there was a great deal of writing about the relationship of handedness and stuttering. It was felt that a lack of hand preference or a change from left to right handedness was the major cause of stuttering. Further research tended to disprove such a direct relationship, but to conclude that a forced change of handedness might be one of the causal factors. Now parents are advised to allow the child to develop handedness on his own, without interference. Although it might be easier to be right handed in our particular society, left handedness should be accepted as a perfectly normal characteristic.

Some people believe that stuttering is caused by a traumatic situation in the early life of the individual. He may have been bitten by a dog, or witnessed the death of his father, or experienced some other harrowing event. But when a complete case history is taken, the fact usually remains that the stuttering was apparent before the shocking experience. Nor is it likely that stuttering is "caught" by imitating someone in the immediate environment, such as a playmate or another member of the family.

Thus far, we have stressed what stuttering is not, or what factors do not cause it. What, then, *does* cause stuttering?

Innumerable theories exist about the genesis of the affliction. (Some of my patients have described their condition as an "affliction.") Many factors probably combine to cause stuttering in any one individual. None of these factors, in itself, would be potent enough to cause a breakdown in speech, but the cumulative effect is disastrous. An understanding of the "multiple causation" basis of stuttering is essential in setting up a program to rid oneself of it. Another way of saying the same thing is that an accumulation of environmental pressures causes stuttering.

Most stutterers say that they have had trouble with their speech as long as they can remember. They may have become acutely aware of it when they were in the upper grades or in high school, but it actually started long before. In many cases the individuals have improved in terms of fluency and then taken a turn for the worse about the time they entered high school. Your speech irregularities may have started

Courtesy of parents.

Fig. 21. Hobbies help to build self-confidence.

when you were four or five; for a time you improved and then at adolescence your speech became more non-fluent.

A beginning point in overcoming your stuttering is "insight" into how and why it began. One authority in the field of speech correction, who was himself a severe stutterer, has stated that the completely happy child will not stutter. So the search begins to find those factors which made your childhood less satisfactory than it might have been. To undertake such an investigation, you must be non-sentimental about your home situation.

Then, too, how you as a child felt about the childhood environment is far more important than how it really was. This last fact explains why two children may be exposed to approximately the same environmental situation and react in entirely different ways. They feel different about it. One stutters and the other doesn't. Or one may have additional pressures which the other one does not experience. No two children, even in the same family, have exactly the same environment. One is older than the other; one is a boy and the other a girl; or one is pretty and the other is not. So we are not particularly interested in how you should have felt about the childhood environment—feeling has little logic; nor are we interested at this point in how you feel about it now. But how did you feel about the environment at that time—at the time you were four, or seven, or fourteen?

None of the factors which we discuss here may apply to your case—but they may suggest areas about which you can think further. So often patients say, "But I never thought about that. I had no idea there was any connection between that and the way I speak." Your speech is a reflection of you. And you are an end product of all the thoughts and feelings which you have ever had. Present attitudes are outgrowths of many years of thinking about and reacting to your immediate surroundings. For all of us, that means our reactions and attitudes towards our family members. So now we are ready to examine more closely some of the factors which made your childhood less ideal.

1. Was your family "normal" in composition?

Did you have both a mother *and* a father living together in a separate dwelling unit? Although divorce is very common today, children still react to it as a direct blow to their security. You may have said nothing about the break-up of the home, but you probably felt it deeply. Perhaps, because you were silent, the wonder and doubt began to come through as a speech problem. The effect of divorce is very likely to be reflected in speech patterns if it occurs when the child is between the ages of three and five.

Additional relatives in the home may lead to complications which jeopardize the child's sense of loyalty to his parents. Any factors which add to his mixed feelings are potential causal factors of stuttering.

The death of the father, although less damaging in its effect than divorce, leaves the family unit disrupted. Some children recover rapidly, but others brood over the loss and are susceptible to emotional states reflected in non-fluent speech.

2. Were your parents happy together?

Even though they may never have quarreled openly in your presence, you were aware of their true feelings. Or, because they were undemonstrative, you may have felt they lacked real companionship. You were afraid that at any time the tensions might explode and you would be homeless. In many cases, the stuttering adults have reported to me that they urged, or wanted to urge their mothers to "get out," to get a divorce.

Happy, well adjusted parents are the keystone to a secure family unit. Overcoming speech problems in children often begins with assisting the parents in solving their problems. As the parents become more relaxed and more accepting of each other, they also become more accepting of the children in their proper perspective as individual, although dependent, units of the family. They no longer need to use the child as a pawn in a battle of the sexes; nor to use the child to supply sympathy and/or affection which should be supplied by each other.

3. Was there competition between or among the children?

So often the stuttering child is one who feels himself losing out in affection within the family. Suppose there were two boys in your family, you and a younger brother. The latter seemed to be more athletic than you, more socially acceptable. He could read faster; he was better in mathematics.

In another case, Charles B — — — — was a year older than Bob. Charles failed in second grade so both boys were in the same class throughout grade school. Bob always got higher grades. Even though their parents never pointed out the difference in their achievements, the fact was all too apparent. In fact, once in fifth grade, a thoughtless teacher remarked, "If you'd try a little harder, you might catch up with your brother Bob." In high school, Bob was an outstanding athlete as well as an honor student and won a scholarship to an Eastern college. Charles, admiring, never complaining, seemed to share Bob's honor; but he stuttered so badly that he could hardly say a complete sentence.

In many instances parents aggravate the home situation by showing favoritism. One woman told me that her father always took her sister's side in every situation. The mother, to keep peace at any price, remained on the sidelines. In many insidious ways the father let Jane know that she was less attractive, less acceptable to him than her sister.

A part of the same picture is comparing children unfavorably to other children within the family, or to neighbor children. Louis har-

Courtesy of Golden Gate Nursery Schools.

Fig. 22. Painting may be a means of expressing
negative emotions.

bored a secret resentment against his mother, who often said, "Why
can't you hang up your clothes like your cousin? Tommy has a paper
route and earns a little money for himself. He comes home right after
school and runs errands for his mother."

4. Did your parents set standards which were too high?

They may have been of the "children are to be seen and not heard"
school. Or they may have punished you severely for the use of socially
unacceptable language. John developed apprehension in terms of

speech because his mother was very nervous and could not stand any noise. He was cautioned constantly to be quiet, not to talk so loud. His father worked at night so the house had to be quiet for him to sleep during the day. Whenever John forgot and talked loud, he was punished; one time his father shouted from the bedroom, "Mary, can't you make that kid keep his mouth shut?" Talking, at least the kind of talking he did, was considered bad. "Good boys are quiet and don't talk needlessly. They censor their language." Because you were not naturally a quiet child and did not always say the right things, you began to hesitate to speak. This fear of saying the wrong thing became more pronounced until others began to remark about your stuttering.

The high standards may have been in areas other than speech. Philip was the son of a lawyer. His mother had been an English teacher before she was married. From his earliest school years they insisted that he stand in the upper third of his class. "It isn't," they would say, "as if we expect you to be the highest." But Philip was only average in academic capacities. Try as hard as he might, he was able to get only a little above average, and sometimes not that. Although his report card showed. "Satisfactory for this child," his parents were never satisfied. He loved his parents, and it made him unhappy to dissappoint them. Every time the report cards came out, he felt a sense of guilt and shame. His stuttering was always worse at these times.

Studies have shown that the mothers of stutterers, as a group, are tense, high-strung, perfectionistic individuals. One speech pathologist facetiously remarked, "If there were no mothers, there would be no stutterers." He did have a point, all right. Mothers, fathers, grandmothers, and old maid aunts who force their unrealistic goals onto children are the precipitating forces behind many stuttering cases. Louise was a nice-looking girl, in a healthly, athletic sort of way. She was fond of animals and the outdoors and wanted to work as a summer camp waitress. Her family thought that well connected young ladies did no such thing. She would go to summer school to make up credits and then enter a girls' finishing school in the fall. This was only one in a series of situations in which Louise's wishes were subordinated to her family's goals for her. If she did not feel herself to be the black sheep of the family, at least she felt that she was the weak link in the chain of generations.

5. *Were your parents consistent in their discipline?*

Were you allowed to do something by one parent and not by another? And if there was a grandmother or an aunt in the home, did she enforce different rules from those of your parents? At the age of three or four, perhaps you were confused about the limits of your activities. Even if you learned to play one parent against the other, you were not really happy about getting your way. There was always the guilty feeling of being found out and punished. In terms of your state of mind, and indirectly in terms of your speech, it would have been preferable to have a few rules which were carried out consistently. Vacillating discipline is worse than severity.

6. *Did you feel that you were fully accepted and loved by your parents?*

It is disastrous for any child to feel that no one, especially his parents, is interested in him. Martin was the son of a traveling salesman. His mother wanted to go with her husband, but found the burden of taking along a child too much. She left him with her parents most of the time; and then, as soon as he was old enough, she sent him to military school. The father lost interest in him completely, and when he and the mother were divorced, disappeared from his life. The mother came to visit him once or twice a year, and allowed him to spend part of the summer vacation with her and the new stepfather. Throughout his school life, Martin's stuttering was a handicap. He began to overcome it only when he got out on his own and developed a life for himself.

7. *Did your parents have considerable financial worries?*

You, as a young child, probably were not directly concerned with financial worries. However, tension over money problems had its effect upon the home. As a sensitive individual, you may have imagined the situation to be even worse than it was. This apprehension was intensified if one or both of your parents were pessimistic about the prospects of the family. Arguments over money may have been held in the presence, or at least within the hearing, of the children.

Ruth was very conscious of their lack of finances. Her earliest memories were concerned with her mother's constant fussing and fuming about what "we can't afford." Ruth was dressed neatly, but her clothes were inferior in quality to those of most of her classmates. Once she complained about wearing "that old brown dress," and her mother gave her a very severe lecture about trying to put on airs. After that, Ruth held her remarks, but her desires to have pretty clothes and trinkets like the other girls caused her great unhappiness. She began to withdraw from the group and to speak with considerable hesitation. When her father got a better job, the money worry was relieved. Gradually, she began to regain her self-confidence and as she did so, her speech improved.

Another related aspect is that of recurrent unemployment. Dale's father had quit school as a high school junior. He had drifted aimlessly until he met and married Dale's mother. Then he began to "settle down," but he was not trained for any occupation. He was also very independent and spoke out against his bosses whenever he felt like it. As a consequence, he was forced to take unskilled labor jobs which were not too much to his liking. He found the work unpleasant and often of a temporary nature. By the time Dale was four, and a stutterer, his father had worked at more than fifteen jobs and the family had moved six times. Dale often asked his father, "Are you going to look for a job today?"

8. *Was your mother a "Mom"?*

We have read a great deal in recent years about "Momism." This term implies the type of woman who hovers over her children, shielding them from every danger, providing them with every comfort. Such a mother sacrifices herself completely for her family; she has almost no interests outside her home. If you were an only child, you received the full force of her devotion. She did not allow you to grow and develop as a normal individual, but waited on you to such an extent that you failed to learn to do things for yourself. You became "spoiled" and found it difficult to make satisfactory contacts with other children. At times you lashed out against this overprotection. And then you felt guilty because you had hurt your mother's feelings. You loved her, but you wished she would let you live your own life. This constant emotional hassel resulted in mixed feelings of liking and disliking. Later, over-protected as you were, you had increasing difficulty in making decisions for yourself. Even as an adult perhaps you cannot break the home ties and are still living with your parents.

9. Did your family make you aware of your speech problem?

Some authorities maintain that you began to stutter simply because someone told you that you stuttered. By calling attention to the fact that your speech was "different," people caused you to retain and carry along a pattern of speech that is perfectly normal during early phases of speech development. Although this explanation fails to take into consideration the numerous possible causes of stuttering, it does stress the importance of other people's attitudes toward your speech. Some persons in your environment, probably your parents, were anxious about your speech and transmitted that anxiety to you. A grandmother, an aunt, or a neighbor may have been the person who made you conscious that your speech was unacceptable.

In addition to making you conscious that your speech was non-fluent, they may also have tried to help you in ways that made matters only worse. "Slow down," "Stop and take a deep breath," "Think before you speak," and similar admonitions only intensified the environmental pressures. For members of the family or others to make fun of the stuttering is especially damaging to the ego. You really would not stutter if you could help it. To call attention to the speech in any way makes the whole situation worse.

As an adult stutterer it may be a comforting thought to realize that you were not responsible for the beginnings of your stuttering. In the primary stage of your speech problem, you were unaware that you were producing speech that differed from that of your playmates. Gradually, however, you became increasingly aware that something was wrong. If the situation had been handled properly at that time, your stuttering might have been "cured." But, unfortunately, that was not so. The attitudes persisted that 1) you would grow out of it, 2) you could speak correctly if you wanted to, and/or 3) you were enjoying the attention you got from stuttering.

As the years went along, you moved on to the secondary stage of stuttering. Now you were fully aware of your speech trouble; you avoided speech situations whenever possible. Many times you said "I don't know" rather than make an effort to answer. You began to withdraw from social groups and to refuse to recite in class. Throughout high school and most of college you had almost no dates because you were afraid to ask a girl. And you wouldn't use the telephone. Social situations became increasingly difficult and you turned to non-speech activities, such as reading or listening to music, for recreation.

Now, as an adult, the stuttering is still with you. It probably is not so bad as it was in your teens, but it is still a major problem, especially on bad days. You have difficulty finding a job because interviews are troublesome. You stick to a job even when you don't like it rather than seek one which will require speaking to the public. You refuse to use the telephone except in emergencies. Finally, you have come to the point where you feel you must do something to overcome this stumbling block.

How can you set about helping yourself to overcome stuttering? The road to control of your speech is a divided highway, requiring a two-pronged approach. You must understand and eliminate, insofar as possible, the causal factors; you must learn new habits of speech which will lead to patterns of fluency.

The most effective emotion in prolonging your stuttering is anxiety or fear. Often a large part of this fear is that people will find out you have trouble with speech. So, step number one, accept your speech as a part of yourself. Really accept it so that you no longer try to hide it. You have, for many years, over-evaluated this problem. As one young lady said to me, "I blame the fact that I am not married onto my speech. In fact, it has been a major obstacle both in the past and at the present time to my success and to my happiness."

Yes, you have a problem, and a serious one. But over a million other people in the United States have the same problem. All right, you do hesitate when you speak. Some people can't see, some can't hear, some can't walk. You merely can't, at this moment, speak as fluently as you would like to. The development of an accepting attitude toward your speech, an objective attitude, is essential to your speech improvement.

Don't hide your stuttering. If you need to hesitate, or to repeat, do so. Begin to eliminate those habits which you have accumulated as devices to keep other people from knowing about your speech. A main offender is substituting. Say the word or phrase you want to say, even if you have a little trouble with it, rather than search for other words. Study your "starters," such as "Well, now—," "Uh—," or "I see, but—," and gradually eliminate them. Say what you want to say without these crutches.

Observing your speech, studying it before a mirror will help you to see yourself as others see you. You may find you have facial mannerisms which detract from what you are trying to say. These may include blinking your eyes, pursing your lips, protruding your tongue, or clenching your teeth. Faulty habits have developed gradually without your being aware of them. Try to speak without these additional facial gestures. Relax the muscles of the face and throat. Let your speech flow out smoothly, rhythmically.

At the same time that you are working on these symptoms which are collectively called stuttering, or non-fluency, you must also achieve a more complete understanding of why this "affliction" has stayed with you all these years. A part of the picture, how the stuttering originally developed, has already been discussed. You must know that circumstances beyond your control, and perhaps anyone's control, caused pressures upon you as a child. Other children in a similar environment would have reacted differently. They might have struck out against obstacles instead of bottling their feelings up inside. Or they might have sucked their thumbs, or had tantrums, or showed their unhappiness in other ways. But your reaction to this unfortunate accumulation of events, pressures, and tensions was to stutter.

Many people have difficulty with the rhythm of their speech. No one lacks hesitancies in his speech; most people have many pauses, repetitions, startings over, and other non-fluencies which are characteristic of the speech of a stutterer. It is all a matter of degree. We could put all people on a continuum so far as fluency is concerned.

```
L_____I_____I_____I_____J
1               2               3               4               5
```

1—Complete blocking; no speech.

2—Borderline. Some people would classify the individual as a stutterer, others would not. The individual himself might or might not think of himself as a stutterer.

3—The average individual, with numerous hesitations, sputterings, and incomplete sentences.

4—The above average person in terms of fluency. Few unplanned pauses or repetitions.

5—Perfect fluency. In fact, the person sounds unnatural; his speech is too smooth, too glib, too polished.

You, as a confessed (or self-evaluated) stutterer, may hover around the #2 position on the continuum. On your good days, you may approach #3 or even #4. The variability of the amount of stuttering may surprise and/or dismay you. One day your speech is very good, and then for no apparent reason, your speech is terrible. Your ups and downs probably follow a pattern, corresponding closely to your emotional cycle, which is fairly consistent. Every two weeks, or two months, or whenever it may be, you hit the top of the emotional crest and your speech is at its best. In between these high points, the speech becomes worse until you hit the lowest point of the cycle.

Now let us expand more fully the #3 position, that of the average speaker. For the most part whenever he wishes to speak, he can do so easily. The need to speak far outweighs any factors which might keep him from speaking. Let's represent this state of affairs by the use of a seesaw.

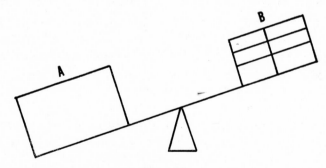

Figure I

A. The need to speak or to use oral communication.

B. Factors which oppose speech.

As you see, "A" is heavier than "B," so that our Mr. Average Speaker has no difficulty. Now if we were to add other factors to side "B," then he would begin to hesitate, to repeat, or to become confused and jumble his speech. For example, suppose Johnny, a boy of fifteen, is very shy around girls. He suddenly finds himself the only boy in a roomful of the fair sex. He may stutter, or sputter a few words, and dash out; or he may rush out without saying anything. The balance of the seesaw has changed.

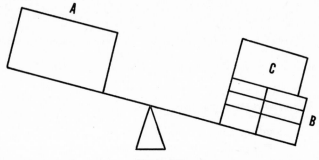

Figure II

The desire to speak has shrunk considerably, and the factors against speaking, especially timidity in the presence of girls (small box "C"), have increased.

Again, Mrs. Brown has no difficulty in speaking in the usual social situation. But she is called upon to introduce the speaker at the Community Club luncheon. Her voice quavers, and she has considerable non-fluency. Many people in Mrs. Brown's position will avoid the situation entirely by refusing to introduce the speaker. They will suggest asking Mrs. King, or Mr. White, or just anyone. She, as many stutterers, solves the problem by running away from it, by avoidance techniques.

If you are Mr. Average Speaker, you may occasionally, at least temporarily, become a #1, or totally blocked individual. Extreme fright or surprise may leave you speechless. You may be taken unaware when asked to make a few remarks at a formal banquet. The need to speak is there, but the factor of fear or surprise is so great that no speech comes out.

So, we see that Speaker #3 on the continuum, Mr. Average Speaker, is not always a non-stutterer. Under certain circumstances, he may become a severe stutterer for a few minutes, or even a few hours. One situation in which he may have a great deal of non-fluency is before an audience in a formal speaking situation. He has stage fright. It may last only a moment, or it may disrupt his entire effort to speak. One girl "froze up" in the middle of her valedictory speech before an audience of classmates and parents; in spite of prompting from the wings, she could not continue, but walked off the stage, completely speechless.

Now you, as an adult stutterer, have a condition similar to chronic stage fright. A very delicate balance exists between your need to speak and the factors which would keep you from speaking. The seesaw looks like this:

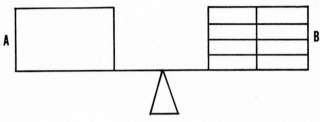

Figure III

On Side A, the forces in favor of speech approximately balance the forces against speaking on Side B. Your speech is good in some situations, such as when you speak as one of a chorus. Speech is also rather fluent when you are motivated by strong emotion, such as anger. In other situations you find it very difficult to speak. Among these may be answering the telephone, giving your name and address, and speaking to people in positions of authority.

In order to make your speech more fluent, you will have to identify and then eliminate, or at least minimize, the bricks (or factors) which are weighing down the balance and blocking your attempts to speak. Just what are the forces which are making it difficult for you to communicate orally? Only you, after a diligent search into your past and a careful analysis of your present circumstances, can answer the question. But we can suggest some of the possibilities.

1. *An unhappy childhood.* We have already discussed in some detail this phase of the problem. It is true that you can do little to change the past, except that you can change your attitude toward it. By understanding others who exerted pressure upon you, you may be able to "forgive" them. One stutterer was particularly bitter against his father who had deserted the family when he was five. As he learned more of the factors which led to the desertion, his hatred of his father diminished. He never forgave him completely, but the hard core of bitterness was softened.

2. *An overemphasis upon your lack of fluency.* That is, you have a self-consciousness about speaking which keeps you from taking advantage of every opportunity to practice. Or when you speak, you use a bag of tricks to cover up, to hide your method of speaking. You avoid words which you think might cause you difficulty. You use starters, such as "Well, now," "Oh, no," or "Just a minute." These and other avoidances are used to keep others from knowing that you stutter. As explained earlier, you must face the problem of stuttering frankly, honestly, and determine to conquer it.

3. *A memory of past failures.* You must regain confidence by having successful experiences which will counterbalance these past failures. You must think of the many times you spoke successfully and not dwell upon the failures. A positive approach is essential. Keep track of the times you succeed. Relive the successes rather than the discouraging situations. When you have been fluent, close your eyes and imagine again just how you felt, how your muscles worked together to produce smooth, easy speech. This recall will help blot out the times that you were not able to say what you wanted to say when you wanted to say it.

4. *Faulty relations with others.* Usually these strained relationships are with members of your immediate family. There is tension with mother, father, or a brother. If so, bring these feelings of hostility out in the open. Find an opportunity to talk things over. Your family may be entirely unaware that you feel the way you do about them. Perhaps you, or they, have misinterpreted certain actions or words. Ease the situation by having a serious, but friendly discussion about the entire matter. If, for example, the handling of money is unsatisfactory, suggest that you work out a budget together.

5. *A general tenseness.* You know that your speech is much better when you are rested and relaxed. Then you must create an atmosphere and a way of life that will allow you to be more rested and more relaxed. Examine the number of activities in which you engage and determine how many of them you can eliminate. Lie down for a few minutes—or sit back in your chair with your eyes closed—two or three times each day. Take more time when you are approaching a situation, especially a feared situation, in which speech is important, such as answering the telephone. Get a reliable book on general relaxation and follow the method suggested. "You Must Relax" by Edmund

Jacobson is a good one. If one book does not satisfy your needs, then try another one.

6. ***Attitudes of dependence.*** This conflict, because every adult needs to have a measure of independence, may set up problems of indecision. You can't decide whether to live at home with your parents or to move away and go on your own. Financial difficulties may enter into the decision and cause you to accept a situation with which you are not entirely happy. You may have a parent, usually the mother, who urges you to stay at home, and because you love her, you give in rather than make her unhappy. This feeling of ambivalence (dependence-independence conflict) may be so strong that you have difficulty in making decisions of any kind. Whether to buy a hat or not to buy a hat becomes a major issue, swollen out of all proportion to its true significance. This indecision is also evident in your speech. The conflict between the need to speak and the desire not to speak causes your speech to flow irregularly, to sputter, to stutter.

Certainly, a very important phase of your therapy—either by yourself or with the help of a trained speech correctionist—is to understand the development of your present pattern of stuttering. One method of seeing this development is to draw a diagram showing your speech at different ages.

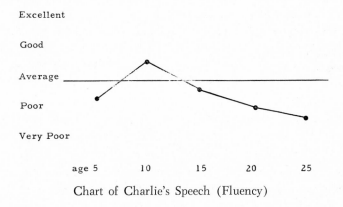

Chart of Charlie's Speech (Fluency)

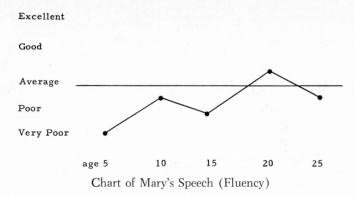

Chart of Mary's Speech (Fluency)

After you have charted the course of your non-fluency, you are ready to try to determine *why* it has fluctuated in severity over the years. What were the circumstances of your life when your speech was "bad"? When it was "good"? What factors were active during the one period or periods which were not active in the other? One patient I had in the clinic discovered that his best speech was during the two years he played professional baseball. Then an injury occurred which ended his baseball career. Almost immediately his speech became non-fluent again during this period of readjustment and search for a new vocational life.

It is not always possible to find a direct connection between the chart and the circumstances of your life, but the investigation may give you leads to follow up. It provides a starting point in self-analysis. What causes stuttering? It is the result of an accumulation of environmental pressures upon an individual personality. To find a permanent "cure," one must unearth the pressures, understand them, and either eliminate them or adjust to them. Overcoming stuttering may be a long, slow process which requires endless hours of self-discipline. But the goal of fluent speech is worth the effort.

Underlying success in any endeavor—whether it is building a business, maintaining a diet, or overcoming stuttering—is the determination to reach the designated goal. Some stutterers have simply made up their minds not to stutter and have ceased to do so. Such a decision and abiding by it requires self-discipline. You probably will not be able to stop stuttering "all of a piece," but you can stop using avoidances, substitutions, and starters. Each day you hack away at the outward symptoms of non-fluency as well as remove causes of tenseness.

"Faith Is The Answer," written by Norman Vincent Peale and Smiley Blanton a few years ago (Dr. Blanton has also written about stutterers.) has much of value for persons whose speech reflects uncertainty. Perhaps the fight to overcome this speech handicap is too much for you to handle alone. Reliance and faith in a power outside yourself may provide the answer. Examine your religious and philosophical concepts. Dedicate yourself to the service of others. One older "cured" stutterer tells me that he made his first appreciable advance in overcoming his handicap when he began to try to help other stutterers. He recommends helping others as a necessary step in the process of speech rehabilitation.

SUMMARY

Stuttering, or non-fluency, is a wide-spread speech handicap. Based on the individual's emotional attitudes in the speaking situation, it can be eliminated only by discovering the underlying causes and finding satisfactory solutions to some of them. At least enough must be handled so that the factors against speaking no longer outweigh the need for oral communication.

Stuttering usually begins when a person is four or five years old. At first he is unaware that he is having speech difficulty until someone calls his attention to it. If the pressures which are causing the stuttering can be removed while he is in this "primary" stage, the individual will probably have a complete "cure." Too often, however, the stuttering progresses to the more severe "secondary" stage when the individual becomes aware of his speech problem and reacts adversely to it.

An adult stutterer will probably never be completely free of non-fluency. But he can learn to control the symptoms and to understand and eliminate certain causal factors. He can become more objective about his stuttering; he can learn to accept it as a relatively unimportant part of himself. By facing the problem of stuttering openly he has made a real beginning in conquering it.

BOOKS TO READ

BRYNGELSON, BRYNG, CHAPMAN, MYFANWY E., AND HANSEN, ORVETTA K.: *Know Yourself*. Minneapolis, Minn., Burgess Publishing Company. 1950.

JOHNSON, WENDELL, *et al.: Speech Handicapped School Children*. New York, Harper, 1948, chap. V.

PEALE, NORMAN VINCENT, AND BLANTON, SMILEY: *Faith Is the Answer.* New York, Prentice-Hall, Inc., 1950.

VAN RIPER, CHARLES: *Speech Correction: Principles and Methods.* New York, Prentice-Hall, Inc., 1944.

VAN RIPER, CHARLES: *Stuttering* (pamphlet). Chicago, Ill., (11 S. La Salle St.) Society for Crippled Children and Adults, Inc., 1948.

WEST, ROBERT, KENNEDY, LOU, AND CARR, ANNA: *The Rehabilitation of Speech.* New York, Harper and Brothers, 1947, chap. IV.

CHAPTER V

YOU WILL SPEAK AGAIN

To: You who must learn esophageal speech

Y our voice box (larynx) was removed to save your life. The operation was successful and the percentages say that you may expect to live your normal life span. It is important to you and those around you that you learn to speak as well as you can.

Before your operation you probably never thought about how you produced speech. All your life—perhaps forty, fifty, or more years— you took speech for granted. You learned to speak so long ago that you forgot that you did so by imitating older people. Now, suddenly, you are completely without speech. For the first time since infancy you are unable to say a word.

Most of your speech equipment is just as it was before the operation, all of it above the throat. But there has been a very fundamental change: The mechanism for producing tone has been removed. These diagrams will clarify this point:

BEFORE

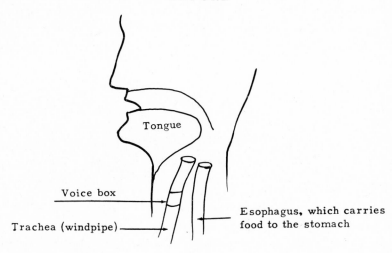

AFTER

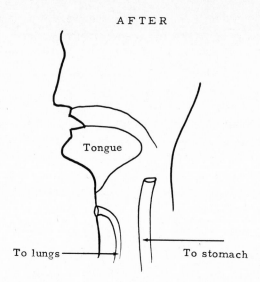

Before the operation, you breathed through your nose and the air went down the trachea, or windpipe, to the lungs. Then, on its way out, the air caused the edges of the vocal cords within the voice box to vibrate. This vibration produced a sound, or basic tone, which was then shaped into speech by the mouth. Now, the voice box and that part of the windpipe between it and the mouth have been removed by the surgeon. He has turned the remaining end of the windpipe forward so that you breathe through the cannula, or opening in your neck.

When the voice box was removed, speech was lost. But the loss need not be permanent. You can learn to speak again. *That is, if you really want to and are willing to put in the effort which is required.* By hard work over a long period of time, a high percentage of laryngectomized persons have learned to speak well enough to make themselves understood. Although their speech is not as fluent and effective as it was before the removal of the larynx, it is very serviceable. Many of them have returned to former occupations which require good speech—salesmen, ministers, lawyers, and foremen in industry.

The length of time necessary to learn the new way of speaking varies. Some individuals have learned to say a few words within two weeks from the time the doctor gave them permission to begin lessons. Usually it takes longer, anywhere from six weeks to a year. Within six months most laryngectomees who make the effort can make themselves understood under normal circumstances. You can expect to make gradual improvement for two or three years before the limits of achievement have been reached.

You and your family must expect no speech, in fact, no sound at all, from you for the first two or three months after the operation. During this time you should use pencil and paper for communication. Don't whisper. *Don't whisper.* **Don't whisper!** When you whisper, you set up muscle patterns which act against learning to speak with esophageal tone. The activity for whispering is in the front of the mouth and on the lips; for your new speech you will need to control the muscles in the lower part of the throat.

Once the doctor has given you permission, usually from three weeks to two months or more after the operation, you are ready to begin the painstaking job of learning to speak. Don't fool yourself. It will not be easy. It will require many hours of effort, *often without success at first*, in order to master the first steps in learning to speak in the new way, the esophageal way.

Since you no longer have a voice box, you must develop a new place of vibration. These vibrations, once they come, produce the basic tone for speech. No one is sure of the place of these vibrations, but they are probably at or near the opening of the esophagus, the tube which leads from the mouth to the stomach. Until now, this tube was used only to carry food and liquids to the stomach, but it must accommodate itself to an additional set of duties.

The first, the most important, and possibly the most difficult step in learning to speak again is forcing air down into the esophagus. Once the air is swallowed, you must allow it to come up again and produce a tone as it passes the valve at the upper end of the esophagus. This ability to produce an audible burp is basic to your new speech. Forget for the time being any inhibitions against "burping"! Nothing else can be done about speaking until tone is produced.

There are probably many methods of achieving results, but the following outline may be helpful to you.

1. Open your mouth wide.

This position allows air from the outside to be forced into the mouth; you must depend upon the air's rushing in to fill a partial vacuum.

2. Breathe in through the cannula, somewhat deeper than usual.

3. At the same time that you are inhaling, sweep the air back into the mouth with the tongue.

Make one definite movement of the entire tongue and not just a waving or a wagging of the tip of the tongue.

4. At the end of the intake of air, swallow.

Be sure there is a definite swallowing motion. For the first few days you may need to take a few drops of water to help you get a true swallow.

5. Wait.

In a few seconds you will feel the air returning upward in the esophagus. Waiting for the return takes patience, but it will pay off in results. Trying to force the air up is of little value.

6. When you feel the air coming up, hold a piece of cloth over the cannula.

The additional pressure of the air in the lungs helps to produce a louder burp.

7. Open your mouth wide so that the burp can escape easily.

You want to avoid having it dissipate through the nose.

8. Burp.

Try to produce a tone. Any kind of tone is acceptable. At first it may be a mere gurgle in the throat.

9. Remove the cloth from the cannula and breathe out.

You must avoid holding your breath so long that it makes you cough.

This procedure may sound complicated, but it occurs very quickly within the space of ten or fifteen seconds. Later it will not be necessary to think about the sequence of action. The essential steps will become automatic and the others will disappear. For example, once you master the burping technique, you will no longer need to open your mouth so wide, or to hold the air in the lungs by placing a cloth over the cannula.

In the beginning stages, it is helpful to drink coke, carbonated water, or some other gas-producing liquid to amplify the burp. As soon as possible—probably within the first week—such artificial assistance should be discontinued. At first the burp will probably sound

like the "ă" sound in "cat" or the "ŭ" sound in "rug." It will be low in
pitch and possibly rather weak.

At this stage of the learning process, try to produce only one sound,
whatever it is, on a single burp. Repeat the entire process before trying another. The steps, briefly, are these:

1. Open your mouth.
2. Breathe in.
3. Sweep air back in the mouth.
4. Swallow.
5. Wait.
6. Cover the cannula.
7. Open your mouth.
8. Burp.
9. Breathe out.

With most laryngectomees, a great deal of practice is required before an audible burp can be produced. Although some individuals are

Courtesy of Pacific Gas and Electric Company.

This laryngectomee uses his esophageal speech daily in speaking over the
telephone and before audiences.

successful the first time they try, many others have to work at it for several days or weeks. In difficult cases it may take several months. The usual progress is for the patient to make faint sounds at the end of the first week. In two or three weeks he is able to shape the sound into vowels, the second step on the road to intelligible esophageal speech. If the tone is very weak, the volume may be increased by swallowing two or three times before attempting a burp.

Practice about fifteen minutes at a time and then rest for an hour or more. Seven or eight practice periods per day should be sufficient. A little pressure on the abdominal muscles just as the air is coming up the esophagus will help to increase the loudness. Sometimes squeezing the throat muscles with the fingers is helpful. These muscles must learn a new activity and they may not respond immediately. When one begins to learn to play the piano or to type, the muscles of the fingers often move slowly and inaccurately. Later after many hours of practice, they move automatically at a very rapid rate. In like manner, the muscles of the esophagus and the throat learn to contract at the proper time to produce the necessary tone.

This required practice is tiring. If the throat muscles become sore, it may be necessary to discontinue attempts at speech for a few hours, or even a day or so. Too intensive practice may lead to nausea or dizziness. Because you have not learned to control the swallowing of the air, it tends to go all the way down to the stomach. Then, when it comes up, it brings distasteful juices with it. Once complete control of the air is established, it no longer goes so far down the esophagus, but remains toward the upper end.

A word of caution about discouragement: You must not give up practice too easily; persistence is needed to master the technique of burping. Some laryngectomees become disheartened during the beginning stage and give up the entire project. Even after you have obtained a satisfactory tone, you may lose it again. This inability to produce tone, or regressive period, may last for hours or even for days. You must be convinced that the tone will return if you keep on practicing. There may be parts of days, such as mornings, when you get along well and other parts of days when just nothing happens. And the burp, even when it is produced, will often not be under your control. It may come late, even after you have given up hope, or it may escape so rapidly that you don't have time to try for a tone. Whenever it comes, open your mouth wide and let it roll out. Relaxation is vital. Avoid trying too hard. The muscles will do the work for you when they are ready.

Let us assume that you are able to produce a vocalized burp; you get a tone and it is reasonably under control. Now you are ready to begin shaping this tone into vowels. Although we have thirteen vowel sounds and three diphthongs in our English language, the easiest ones to remember are the familiar "ā," "ē," "ī," "ō," "ū." On a separate burp for each one, try these five long vowels. It may help to think of a word for each one as you attempt it: "ache," "each," "ice," "oat," and "uke." Do not try, at first, for the consonant sound at the end, but just the vowel. When you are able to produce the long vowels, continue to the short vowels, those in "ăt," "mĕt," "ĭt," "cŏt," and "ŭp."

When you are able to make these sounds, you are well on your way toward speech, you should learn the proper shape for each of the vowels so you will be prepared for the burp. If you wait until the burp comes, it will probably escape before you can produce the vowel. This listing of the vowels may help you:

ē (key)	ōō (coupe)
ĭ (kit)	ŏŏ (cook)
ā (cake)	ō (coat)
ĕ (keg)	ô (cough)
ă (cat)	ä (car)
ŭ (cup)	er (cur)

You are now ready for a listener. You think that you are making a certain vowel, but your listener does not agree with you. After all, the listener is the one who must understand what you say. Perhaps you are muffling the sound with too much wind coming out of the cannula, or you are distorting the basic tone. Here again, much practice is demanded on your part so that you can hit the vowels precisely. Try first one of the vowels and then another and let your listener determine if you succeeded. When you have gained enough control over the burp to produce most of the vowels, you are ready to progress to the next step.

It is important to get good placement of the tone early in the learning process. Probably the best consonant to use for this purpose is "k." The words used in the vowel list are indicated for such practice.

You can also use "g" as the beginning consonant: gate, gas, goat, etc. You might also add the three diphthongs (two vowels said so closely together that they sound like one), as in "cow," "kite," and "boy."

After some practice on this step, try various words of one syllable. Return to practice on the vowels from time to time. Good speech will depend upon your being able to hit any vowel or diphthong precisely without undue effort. The vowels are the backbone of speech. Practice them diligently. Counting to ten, one number per burp, is good material. Letters of the alphabet may be utilized in the same way.

One syllable words for practice:

1. ouch	11. no	21. man
2. ape	12. yes	22. bus
3. oak	13. boy	23. ring
4. itch	14. rain	24. scat
5. ax	15. pup	25. box
6. up	16. chew	26. fine
7. egg	17. top	27. road
8. earth	18. ball	28. my
9. odd	19. back	29. but
10. eye	20. door	30. mud

For some laryngectomees, practice is difficult unless they imagine a scene in which they would be using speech. They find it more useful to imagine themselves answering a question. For example:

1. What is your first name?
2. How many children do you have?
3. What is your wife's first name?
4. What do you like most for breakfast?
5. What is your son's name?
6. In what month did you have your operation?
7. What day of the week is this?
8. Do you prefer coffee, tea, or milk?
9. How do you feel today?
10. How many rooms are there in your house?

As soon as you have accomplished a number of one-syllable words, you should try to do two syllables on one burp. Counting is helpful in extending the time you can phonate on one air bubble. Swallow, then say "one-two"; swallow, "three-four"; swallow, "five-six"; etc. You may utilize letters of the alphabet in the same way. Swallow, "a-b"; swallow, "c-d"; swallow, "e-f"; etc. The numbers between 10 and 100, the names of the days of the week and the months of the year are good for practice.

Use additional practice material at this step. First say the words separately, each on a different burp as indicated by the slant mark. Then, as soon as you can, say both words on a single air bubble. If the air bubble isn't large enough, swallow two or even three times before attempting to say the words.

1. Go / home.	11. Cook / meat.
2. Sit / down.	12. Cheer / up.
3. Come / in.	13. Get / out.
4. Shake / hands.	14. Right / now.
5. Good / bye.	15. Fine / day.
6. Call / me.	16. I / know.
7. Pay / day.	17. Take / care.
8. Look / out.	18. Walk / fast.
9. Don't / go.	19. Pardon / me.
10. Keep / calm.	20. Good / night.

With each step you will need to check your progress with a listener. In fact, you are now ready to try to communicate orally with persons outside the home. A trip to the grocery store will give you an opportunity to try "bread," "meat," etc. Or you may greet old friends with "Hello." There will probably be no "h" sound at the beginning of the word; "h" is one of the most difficult sounds to produce. Many laryngectomees never accomplish it, but must remain "cockneys" for the rest of their lives. You can make yourself understood very well without the "h" sound.

A serious problem in articulation is the voicing of whispered consonants. In English, there are eight pairs of consonants which are made just alike except that one member of the pair is voiced (has tone) and the other is whispered (has no tone). Unless the laryngectomee is very careful, he will fail to make the difference noticeable. Special exercises are necessary to call your attention to this difficulty.

Whispered	*Voiced*
1. pie	buy
pig	big
pin	bin
pill	Bill
pear	bear
peat	beat
2. tie	die
tan	Dan
toe	doe
tell	dell
time	dime
tuck	duck
3. coat	goat
could	good
came	game
call	gall
cat	gat
card	guard
4. fail	vale
fan	van
fine	vine
face	vase
feign	vain
fairy	very
5. thigh	thy
ether	either
bath	bathe
teeth	teethe
breath	breathe
cloth	clothe
6. seal	zeal
sink	zinc
seek	Zeke
fuss	fuzz
bus	buzz
loose	lose

	Whispered	*Voiced*
7.	chump	jump
	cheep	jeep
	chest	jest
	choke	joke
	chug	jug
	chunk	junk

8. This pair does not lend itself to matched words, but examples are as follows:

*sh*oe	mea*s*ure
ru*sh*	rouge

Now, try two or three words on one burp. At first say each word on a separate burp; then the first word on one burp and the second and third words on the second burp; as soon as possible do all three words on one burp.

Sentences for practice:

1. Light / the / candle.
      Light / the candle.
            Light the candle.

2. Take / the / picture.
      Take / the picture.
            Take the picture.

Use the identical pauses for the following sentences:

3. Catch the ball.
4. Cross the street.
5. Comb your hair.
6. Dust the chair.
7. Light the fire.
8. Wash your face.
9. Wave the flag.
10. Write a letter.
11. Feed the cat.
12. Tie your shoe.
13. Set the clock.
14. Milk the cow.
15. Ride the horse.
16. Take your lunch.
17. Save your money.
18. Play the piano.
19. Pass the bread.
20. Stop the car.
21. Wipe the dishes.
22. Take the bus.
23. Strike a match.
24. Nail it shut.
25. Thank the man.

Longer sentences come next. The phrasing is indicated by the slant marks. As you increase the number of words you can say on one burp, you will be decreasing the number of phrases. The phrasing should make sense. If you pause in unnatural places, the listener will have difficulty in understanding you.

Examples for practice:
1. Let's go / to the show.
2. Put out / the cat.
3. Take off / your coat.
4. Why don't / we go / for a walk?
5. Please pass / the bread / to me.
6. I want / to go / to the store.
7. I'd like / a cup / of coffee.
8. To improve / your speech / practice / many hours.
9. The window / was broken / when the boys / threw a ball / at it.
10. The floor / was covered / with papers / but the man / walked out / of the room.

You may gain additional practice by reading aloud from the daily newspapers or from a magazine. Keep the length of the phrase short enough to maintain tone throughout. If you lose the tone at the end, you are trying to say too much on one burp.

For the most part volume will develop automatically. As you practice and improve in fluency, the air bubble in the esophagus will gradually enlarge. This additional capacity will allow for more power behind your speech. You can help the process by taking two or three swallows before producing a tone, and thus building up the amount of air locked in the air pocket, or air bubble. You can also increase the volume by contracting the abdominal muscles at the front of the stomach to push the air out more forcibly.

There is need for education of the public regarding esophageal speech. Most people are surprised when they hear it for the first time. You can help them by explaining in simple terms why your new speech is different. If the listener has difficulty in understanding you, assume that you are not being as clear as you should be. Speak slowly. Continue through a phrase without repeating any words. If the listener does not understand, start over and go straight through again.

If he still has difficulty, try different words; perhaps some of the sounds are too difficult for you. Be patient. Sometimes it will be necessary to write your words down for the listener.

One of the aids to learning to speak again is to hear others who have learned esophageal speech. Many of the larger cities now have local chapters of the International Association of Laryngectomees. In San Francisco the "Lost Chord Club" meets monthly as a social group. The members encourage each other in perfecting their speech and in making the many other adjustments necessary following a laryngectomy. No one understands the problems of the laryngectomee better than those who have been through the same experience.

A small percentage of laryngectomized individuals are unable to learn esophageal speech. Factors which make it more difficult to learn are advanced age, extensive surgery, and lack of proper instruction. For these persons, as a last resort, mechanical aids are available. The speech produced by these aids is less lifelike than esophageal speech, but it is certainly preferable to remaining mute.

Two such aids are sold commercially. One is the electro-larynx, made by the Aurex Corporation, Chicago, Illinois. With it the user must carry batteries and a vibrator. He holds the vibrator under his chin or at the side of his throat. Tone is thus transmitted to the mouth cavity where it may be shaped into speech.

The other commercial aid is the Western Electric artificial larynx. The 2AA Artificial Larynx is low-pitched and is designed for men; the 2BA has a higher pitch and is made especially for women. Even with the artificial aid a certain amount of instruction is important. Many hours of practice are necessary before controlled speech is possible. It is well to remember, however, that the speech thus produced lacks the pitch changes of the normal voice.

SUMMARY

Developing effective esophageal speech is a long-term process. Although you may be speaking intelligibly in a few weeks, you can expect improvement for at least the first three years. You must practice each step in learning this new skill. Don't hurry, but seek occasions to use your new speech. Strangers, as well as members of your family, are anxious to help you when they understand why your speech is different from the normal. You need feel no embarrassment in talking, either socially or in the business world. After you have gained some proficiency, most people will think that you have a bad cold and will probably not give your speech additional thought.

BOOKS TO READ

DOEHLER, MARY A.: *Esophageal Speech* (Manual for Teachers). Boston 16, Mass. (462 Boyleston St.), American Cancer Society, Inc. (Massachusetts Division), 1953.

NELSON, CHARLES R.: *You Can Speak Again.* New York, Funk and Wagnalls Company, 1949.

CHAPTER VI

REBUILDING LANGUAGE
(STROKE CASES)

To: The wife of a man who has had a stroke

Your husband, John, was one of the leading business men of your community. He was always active and aggressive—a hard worker, a "go-getter." Although he was a financial success, he was a worrier. He could never take time out for relaxation. Some people found him a little hard to work for; he expected too much. And then—last year, at fifty, he had a stroke.

For the first few weeks John was paralyzed on the right side, and he had no speech. Within the first six months there was a gradual improvement physically. A physiotherapist came in twice a week to give him exercises for his leg and arm. Now, ten months later, he is able to walk with a cane. His greatest difficulty is with speech. He can't say what he wants to say. He seems to know what he wants to say, but he just can't get the words out.

He should have professional help in regaining his oral language. You have inquired, and there is no speech therapist in your community who has had experience with aphasia (loss of the ability to use language). John refuses to leave home to stay at a rehabilitation center. There is none close enough for him to be an out-patient.

Your children are grown. You and John are alone, so you have plenty of time to help him with his language recovery. I do not say speech recovery, because all the aspects of language—listening, speech, reading, and writing—are interrelated. As you are able to improve one of these aspects of language, there will probably be improvement in the others. But you must get busy; *the longer you wait, the more difficult the process of recovery becomes.*

You must realize that you are getting into a long and involved undertaking. Recovery of language takes many months or even years. No one can predict whether a given individual will make progress.

No one knows just how much progress he will make toward his former ability in communication. Authorities on the subject believe that he should have an intensive program of language training for five to six hours every day. I tell you this to make you understand how slow progress may be. But there is hope, and in many cases the patient does regain most of his former ability. In other cases, he at least learns, or re-learns, enough to get by. In some cases, unhappily, there seems to be little or no return of language facility.

A beginning point is to find out how much spoken language John can understand. Give him simple directions to see if he can comprehend and carry them out:

1. Point to your eye, nose, shoes, etc.
2. Hand me the book.
3. Put the cup on the table.
4. Close the door.
5. Turn on the light.
6. Raise your right hand.
7. Bring me the scissors.
8. Move the blue chair from the corner to the center of the room.
9. Put your glasses on the second shelf of the bookcase.
10. Turn the television off and then open the window in the kitchen.

You may need to use gestures as you explain what you want him to do. Or you may have to show him how to carry out the directions by doing them for him. Then ask him to do the same thing. These directions are used to find out whether he can hear and understand when you talk to him.

Does John have any speech at all? Can he name objects in the room—lamp, chair, table, rug, window, etc.? Can he give his name and address? Can he count up to ten? He may answer all questions with the same phrase, such as "I use my eyes," or more likely a swear word. It is very common for him to perseverate with one phrase, that is, continue with the same answer to several questions. It sounds as though the needle were stuck in a broken record. Usually, it is best to wait for a minute or more before asking the next question.

If he has little or no difficulty on this level of speech activity, try simple conversation. Ask him what he has been doing today. Can he form sentences? Ask him to tell you about his favorite sport. Is he able to relate a sequence of ideas? Ask him to tell about some recent family happening.

Three other areas remain to be checked. They may not seem to be directly related to speech, but they are very important. These are the three "R's": reading, writing, and arithmetic. Can he read simple words? Simple sentences? The newspaper? Is he able to read aloud the main words (nouns and verbs) although he still mixes up the little ones, such as "in," "of," (prepositions); "and," "but" (conjunctions); and "a," "the" (articles). In writing, (with the left hand if the right is paralyzed), can he put down a simple sentence which you dictate to him, such as "I want to go to the movie"? If this is too difficult, can he copy it if you write it out for him? When he writes, does he spell correctly? Can he do simple elementary arithmetic? Adding, subtracting, multiplying, and dividing?

You now have a picture of the language ability of your husband. It is theoretically possible that he may be able to read even though he cannot speak—or that his writing ability will not be affected. It is our experience, however, that losses occur in all the symbolic functions, including both language and mathematics. Later certain areas may be more advanced because they have received more attention in the retraining program or because of the aptitude of the patient. You will want to write down a summary statement of John's abilities. It forms a basis of comparison to check progress in another six months or a year.

For instance:

Listening: Understands simple directions when given slowly.

Speaking: Can say only his name and count up to ten.

Reading: Can point to the correct word in a list of the names of common objects.

Writing: Can copy simple words, but no writing on his own.

Mathematics: Can recognize numbers up to ten.

Many factors will enter into the possibilities of a successful program of language recovery. Among them are age and sex. The younger the patient, the more likely he is to respond. Your husband, at fifty, is a relatively young man. Persons in their seventies are less apt to make significant progress. In general, women seem to respond to treatment more favorably than men. Perhaps this is a continuation of the tendency for girls to be more proficient in language than boys. At any rate, women seem to be more willing to do the sort of drill work that is required for recovery. Men, too often, are impatient and refuse to carry out a regular series of exercises. The important thing is to get started. Set aside a regular time for speech lessons. They might be half an hour in length, three times each day.

Very important to the probability of success is John's general physical condition. If he has been or is making a good physical recovery, his chances of regaining language are very good. Physical and occupational therapy should be continued as long as they are effective. The extent of the brain damage is another important factor; your consulting neurologist can give you helpful information on this point. There is really nothing you can do about this factor, but you can be realistic in terms of the goals you set for yourself and for your husband. You can see to it that he gets plenty of rest, that the tempo of your home is calm, and that he has proper food.

Again we must stress that the process of getting back language is a long and often discouraging one. It may take weeks or even months of effort before any significant advance is made. On the other hand, advances are likely to be retained if there is no further physical difficulty. A vital factor all along is to maintain the morale of both yourself and your husband. If the lessons are planned so that the patient has some success each time, the program will go forward at maximum efficiency. When either the patient or the therapist becomes discouraged, a new approach should be made. This may be the point at which the services of a trained speech correctionist must be utilized.

You have found out what ability in using his language your husband possesses at the beginning of the program. Where do you begin in helping him to recover as much as possible? You will not be teaching him anything entirely new, but trying to reawaken former speech and language patterns. The belief of research workers is that another part of the brain takes over the function of the injured area. It is as though a severe storm had struck a complicated telephone system. Direct connections from one major city to another distant city have been disrupted. New and possibly very round-about pathways must be discovered. All means of reawakening the old associations must be employed. No one knows what actually takes place in the brain; we

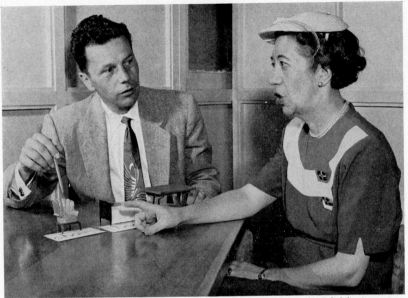

Courtesy of Morrison Center for Rehabilitation.

Fig. 32. "Ch" is a difficult sound to produce.

can judge only by results. Your husband either does or does not learn to speak again.

By regarding the recovery of language as a speech problem and by following the suggestions given in the first three chapters of this book, you can help to build up the use of language. Although there are many differences between a child's learning to speak and your husband's learning to speak again, constant speech stimulation is vital. You must regard yourself as a speech model for him. Speak slowly and in simple language. Repeat the names of objects, such as table, chair, spoon, coffee, as you normally contact them. Explain their uses in simple words, and demonstrate when possible. Remember that your student is an adult. You might think of him as a foreigner who is having his first contact with English. Since you do not know his language, you must make yourself understood by repeating over and over again the names of objects until he can produce them. He will be able to retain nouns and verbs first. Then come their modifiers, the adjectives and adverbs, "pretty," "big," "swiftly," "Take it easy." The more difficult words to speak and to write are the connecting words, the conjunctions, "if," "although"; the prepositions, "in," "under," "behind";

and the words which take the place of nouns, the pronouns, "he," "they," "ourselves." This order of learning words is much the same for the child, the foreigner learning a new language, and the aphasic.

In addition to this general language approach, you will want to try teaching him how to articulate the individual sounds. Chapter III explains in detail how this is done, and there are lessons for all the sounds of English in the Appendix. When he is having difficulty on a particular sound, such as "f," you can spend additional time and drill on it. You can ask him to watch you make the sounds and then imitate what he sees and hears. With some patients an intense program in lip reading is beneficial if a teacher is available. This approach is more successful in those cases classified as expressive aphasia. Here the patient understands language and knows what he wants to say, but he has difficulty in forming the words. As one woman explained to me, "I know what I want to say, but it doesn't come out right."

Many cases, however, do not respond readily to a "Say what I say" approach. They have receptive aphasia; that is, they do not understand language in the first place. They live in a world of incoming jargon and jibberish. Once they get the idea and translate it into words, they can say it. There is no paralysis of the muscles of articulation or of the voice box. (In such cases, starting from the beginning in building up language again is essential.) Their loss is such that they often respond better through visual rather than auditory channels. Their sight is more receptive than their hearing. Although you continue to repeat words and to build up oral language in every way possible, the stress is on reading and other visual materials. Writing of words and numbers becomes an integral part of the exercise materials.

You may need to begin with pre-reading or reading readiness materials. A first step is to get the patient to match identical pictures. Because adults have been using pictures and printed materials for many years, they often succeed more easily with them than with the objects themselves. Place three or four pictures of common objects on the table before your husband. Give him an identical picture of one of them. Then explain in words, or by demonstration, just what you want him to do. Say, "Where is the same picture?" "Where is the house?"

When he can match identical pictures with some degree of success, proceed to the next stage of identification. Put four pictures in front of him and ask him to point to the one which you name; for example, "cat." If he fails to respond within ten seconds, show it to him as you say the name. Then repeat the name and ask him to point to it. You may need to repeat the request several times. His memory may be so short that he cannot remember long enough to reach for the picture.

The important thing at this stage is to build up a vocabulary of the names of objects. Take him on a tour of the house, pointing out such things as chair, table, window, light, etc. Say each name several times and get him to repeat it if he will. Have him watch your face as you say the word. Use the name in a short sentence, as "We sit on a *chair*," "I can turn on the *light*." Also give an incomplete sentence and allow him time to supply the final word:

1. We sit in a ———.
2. Turn on the ———.
3. I must sweep the ———.
4. We eat at a ———.

It is often helpful to give him the first sound of the missing word:

1. We sit in a ch——.
2. Turn on the li——.
3. I must sweep the fl——.
4. We eat at a ta——.

The training of memory span is often a definite part of the rehabilitation program. A simple test is to ask him to carry out directions. Start with one request, as "Please close the door." If he is willing and able to cooperate, you can give him increasingly more complicated directions. For example, "Put this book on the table, close the drawer of the desk, and bring me the magazine from the rack." Further memory training may be somewhat more formalized. Say numbers below ten at the rate of one per second. Try two numbers first and ask him to repeat them. If he succeeds, go on to three numbers, then to four, etc., until you reach his limit. You may ask him to repeat the numbers in reverse; that is, when you say "one-seven-nine," he is to say "nine-seven-one." Gradually he may increase his memory span to six or seven digits. It is very difficult for an individual to use words of four or five syllables if he has a memory span of only three digits.

Although you must be careful in the use of infantile materials, some patients will participate in game situations. One which aids in memory building is this: Put three objects (or more) under a box. Remove the box for ten seconds. Recover them and ask the patient to name all the objects. Increase the number of objects until you reach his limit. Do memory span exercises ten or fifteen minutes each day.

As soon as possible you may start using printed words along with the pictures. Some patients can read the words even before they can identify the pictures. Begin by having a combination of picture and word cues. Spread out four word cards in front of him, and then hand him a picture-word card with one of the words. Ask him to read the word for you by matching it. (See illustration, opposite page.)

Even if he has no speech, he may be able to do the matching. If four words are too confusing, use only two. When he does the matching with four easily, increase the choice to six or eight. Say the words which you hand to him, especially if he has no speech, so that he can begin to associate the picture, the spoken word, and the printed symbol. In cases where this is reasonably convenient, you might also add the real object, such as a book, fork, hat, etc. The idea is to get as many stimuli working together in trying to re-awaken the names of things.

When he can identify words from pictures, at least a part of the time, you may start using a child's dictionary for reading practice. Turn to any page and call one of the pictured words. Instruct the pa-

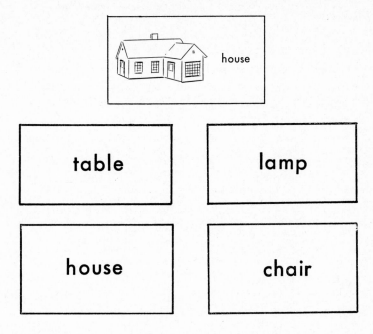

tient to point to the illustration, saying the word at the same time. Then ask him to read the sentence which accompanies the picture. If he cannot, you may read it first and then ask him to repeat it. Another method is to have him read it with you. He may miss all the words, but he is working toward the rhythm of normal speech. As you repeat the sentence a second or third time, drop out on one of the key words and indicate that he is to supply it. Don't repeat the same sentence more than four or five times, or he will become bored with the exercise. Turn to another page and repeat the procedure.

Writing should be introduced as soon as possible in the re-learning process. As you are showing the object or a picture of it, and saying its name, add the writing of the word. Your husband then sees the object, says its name, sees the name in print, and writes. Sometimes patients are able to write the word even before they can say it. When your patient attempts to say something and fails, you can suggest that he write it down. The left hand should be used in writing. *Even though the right hand is not paralyzed, authorities recommend the use of the left hand.* In the case of right-handed persons, injury to the left side of the brain caused the speech loss. Therefore, the opposite side of the brain, the right side, which controls the left hand, should be built up. Of course, the reverse is true with left-handed individuals.

You may write the word first, or print it if he seems to prefer printing. Ask him to copy the word. If he cannot, you may guide his hand for him. Be sure the paper is placed at the proper angle for left-handed writing.

Say the word as you write it. Get him to say it as he writes. When concentration or effort on the writing is too great and absorbs too much of his attention, you may have to wait and have him say the word just after he has written it. Numbers up to ten may prove to be easier for him than words. It may take several days, weeks, or even months before he can write anything from dictation instead of copying it.

If your husband continues to be unable to pronounce words, more and more emphasis should be placed on reading and writing. Build up the "intake" side of language through hearing and reading. Let writing serve as the "expressive" side. Speech will come, if it does, as a by-product of the general language program. You may use word-picture cards in the next stage of reading. Using the key words from the cards, write simple sentences incorporating them. Place four of the sentences before the patient; read one of them aloud and ask him to identify which one you read. If he makes mistakes, place the word-picture before him as an added clue.

At first he may need your help to identify the correct sentence. You are not asking him to read with meaning, but merely to recognize the

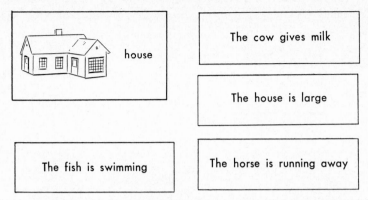

key word used in a sentence. Say, "Hand me the sentence which says, 'The house is large.'" As soon as he can identify the correct sentence with the help of the word-picture card, you can try the exercises without the added clue. If he can pick out the correct sentence rather consistently, you may be assured that he is beginning to associate the spoken word with the printed symbols. He is beginning to read.

A similar procedure can be used with simple arithmetic problems:

Here the card which you hold is to be matched with the proper one

$$4+2=6$$
$$3+2=5 \qquad 4+2=6$$
$$2+5=7 \qquad 2+1=3$$

of the four in front of your husband. Read the card for him and ask him to find the one just like it. He may be able to do so even though he cannot count to ten or recognize the use of the numbers in any way. Other simple problems employing subtraction, multiplication, or division give variety.

In a few cases the power to solve mathematical problems returns more quickly than other abilities. If your husband can do this, capitalize on his ability. Success is good for his morale. Get an elementary mathematics text and give him regular assignments from it. Spend a part of his lesson going over the problems. It is better to try the language activities first and then "relax" with the area in which he is more successful.

The next step in your program may be with pictures from magazines. Published materials may be too infantile to hold the attention of the adult aphasic. You will have to make up materials for him according to his interests. Start with very simple situations and go to more complex ones as he is able to understand them. Under the picture which you have pasted on a piece of typing paper, print a brief question or incomplete statement followed by two or three possible answers.

Courtesy of San Francisco Examiner.

Fig. 54. Picture of bear.

1. What is in the picture?
   bear   house   cat
2. What is he doing?
   sleeping   eating   trees
3. Bears like to drink ....
   milk   dishes   table

Discuss the picture first. Mention what the animal is and what he is doing. Then after you have prepared him for the subject matter, read the first question to him. Ask him to indicate which word of the possible choices is correct. The first time you may need to point to the word and name it. As he gets the idea of what you want him to do, he will be able to point to it without additional help.

Courtesy of San Francisco Examiner.

Fig. 55. Picture of sheep.

1. These animals are ....
    horses   sticks   sheep

2. The baby is called a ....
    lamb   calf   ladder

3. How many animals are there in the picture?
    six (6)   three (3)   ten (10)

4. How many lambs are there in the picture?
    eight (8)   three (3)   one (1)

5. Sheep are raised to produce ....
    cheese   wool   lumber

As he becomes a little more adept, you may add a few sentences of description under the picture and then put the questions or completion sentences on a separate sheet of paper.

Courtesy of San Francisco Examiner.

Fig. 56. Picture of monkey.

A favorite animal of both children and adults is the monkey. He entertains with his funny actions. In this picture we see two monkeys. One is sitting on the branch of a tree; the other is swinging on a rope. One end of the rope is attached to a large bell. Do you think it would be interesting to have a monkey for a pet?

1. The animals in the picture are ....
    cows   monkeys   chimneys

2. One of them is holding onto a ....
    tooth   lamp   rope

3. They may be trying to ring the ....
    tree   bell   ladder

4. Some people have monkeys as ....
    carpets   pets   dishes

5. These monkeys have long ....
    necks   fences   tails

Courtesy of San Francisco Examiner.

Fig. 57. Picture of lion.

The lion is known as the King of the Jungle. He is a large and fierce member of the cat family. Big game hunters go on safaris to Africa to track him down. The lion has appeared prominently in movies about the jungle. In some children's stories he has been depicted in a comic role, such as the Cowardly Lion. In the United States we see him only in the circus or the zoo.

1. The native home of the lion is _____.
2. An enemy of the lion is _____.
3. Sometimes he is a star of _____.
4. If we want to see a lion, we must go to _____.
5. A baby lion is called a _____.

Singing may be a useful medium of recalling words. Many aphasics have sung their first words rather than spoken them. Get your husband to join in with you in singing some of his old favorites. Other automatic speech responses should be utilized, such as "Hello," "I'm fine," "Thank you," and "Goodbye." Church rituals, such as the Lord's Prayer, can be helpful in getting a start on speech. Have him join in with you in choral speaking fashion. Time tables, the alphabet, days of the week, months of the year, and Mother Goose rhymes may give him confidence in trying speech. The automatic speech responses are much easier for him than conversational speech. He might be able to say all of these and still not be able to formulate and express an idea on his own. But they provide a starting point for oral communication.

Always get him to participate in reading, writing, and speaking. He must take an active part in the program. One learns to swim by swimming; you could stand on the bank and watch others swim all your life without learning to swim yourself. The same applies to re-learning how to speak. Listening to the radio or watching television is enjoyable and relaxing. It may have a certain value in gaining background experience with language, but it does not teach your husband to use the other aspects of language himself. Nothing can be worse than to allow him to slip into an accepting attitude so that he no longer tries to learn. Although one must be realistic in the amount of progress expected, the drive for learning to speak again must be kept alive.

When your husband has progressed to reading and understanding on the third-grade level (See workbooks listed at close of chapter), you can begin to use some of the published series of reading lessons. They are well written and graded in difficulty. The most varied one as to subject matter is the Reader's Digest Reading Skills Series. The material begins on the third-grade level and continues through the sixth. Questions are given at the end of each article. Shorter selections are given in the Crabbs-McCall series and in the Grover series. Other such series may be obtained by writing to the publishers of school texts.

SUMMARY

An increasing number of middle-aged persons are victims of CVA, cerebral vascular accidents, or strokes, every year. Usually there is paralysis of one side and some involvement of the language facility. For the first six months there may be spontaneous recovery; after that, further progress will probably require occupational, physical, and speech therapies. No one, at this time, can predict how far along the road to speech and language recovery the patient may travel. According to Longerich and Bordeaux in "Aphasia Therapeutics" (page 96), prognosis for the aphasic patient depends upon six major factors:

1. The premorbid psychological, intellectual, and educational backgrounds.
2. The age and general health of the patient.
3. The site and severity of the neurological injury.
4. The institution of therapy as soon as possible after the cerebral insult.
5. The aphasic's will to improve.
6. The attitude of the family toward the patient.

Unfortunately, in many localities there are no speech therapists who have been trained to work with brain-damaged patients. Retraining may have to be done by family members. Even under the best conditions, recovery is likely to be a long and tedious process. Language retraining should be started as soon as possible after the stroke and continued as long as there is any hope of response. Many victims of strokes have regained all or nearly all of their former ability to speak, read, and write. Working with aphasics, especially by family members, requires great patience and persistence. There is need for variety of approach to cut down on the boredom of repetition; there is need for real interest and enthusiasm on the part of the "teacher" to incite a will to improve on the part of the patient. Many are the stroke victims who begin language rehabilitation, but few are they who persist to ultimate victory. But remember: *Improvement in language ability is worth the price to achieve it.*

BOOKS TO READ

BACKUS, OLLIE: *Aphasia in Adults.* Ann Arbor, Mich., University of MICHIGAN Press, 1946.

GARDNER, WARREN H.: *Left-Handed Writing, Instruction Manual.* Danville, Ill., The Interstate Press, 1945.

LONGERICH, MARY C., AND BORDEAUX, JEAN: *Aphasia Therapeutics.* New York, The Macmillan Company, 1954.

WEST, ROBERT, KENNEDY, LOU, AND CARR, ANNA: The Rehabilitation of Persons with Aphasia, in *The Rehabilitation of Speech.* New York, Harper and Brothers, 1947, chap. 25.

MATERIALS

DOLCH, E. W.: *Picture-Word Game* (box of picture-word cards). St. Louis, Mo., The Hart Vance Company.

McCALL, WILLIAM, AND CRABBS, LELAH MAE: *Standard Test Lessons in Reading.* New York, Bureau of Publications, Teachers College, Columbia University.

MORRIS, ELIZABETH: *Adult Adventures in Reading.* New York, E. P. Dutton and Company.

READER'S DIGEST: *Reading Skill Builders* (eight books). Pleasantville, New York, The Reader's Digest Educational Service, Inc.

STONE, CLARENCE R., AND GROVER, CHARLES C.: *Practice Readers* (Books 1-4). Los Angeles, Cal., Webster Publishing Company.

APPENDIX

The lessons in the Appendix are designed to give basic materials for each of the sounds in the English language. Detailed instructions for using the lessons are presented on pages 44 to 48 in Chapter III.

The order of the lessons corresponds to the difficulty of production of the sounds and to the order in which they are learned by children. The vowels, which are normally easier to make than the consonants, are given first. The most difficult sounds, such as "r" and "s," are near the end of the series.

Books with additional material for children:

ANDERSON, VIRGIL A.: *Improving the Child's Speech.* New York, Oxford University Press, 1953.

NEMOY, ELIZABETH McGINLEY: *Speech Correction Through Story Telling Units.* Magnolia, Mass., Expression Company, 1954.

SCOTT, L. B., AND THOMPSON, J. J.: *Talking Time.* St. Louis, Mo., Webster Publishing Company, 1951.

WOOD, ALICE E.: *Sound Games.* New York, E. P. Dutton and Company, 1948.

WOOD, ALICE E.: *The Jingle Book of Speech Correction.* New York, E. P. Dutton and Company, 1934.

ZEDLER, EMPRESS YOUNG: *Listening for Speech Sounds.* Garden City, N. Y., Doubleday and Company, Inc., 1955.

Books with additional material for adults:

ANDERSON, VIRGIL A.: *Training the Speaking Voice.* New York, Oxford University Press, 1942.

BRIGANCE, W. N., AND HENDERSON, FLORENCE M.: *A Drill Manual for Improving Speech.* New York, J. B. Lippincott Company, 1945.

FAIRBANKS, GRANT: *Voice and Articulation Drillbook.* New York, Harper and Brothers, 1940.

HAHN, ELISE, *et al.: Basic Voice Training for Speech.* New York, Mc Graw-Hill Book Company, 1952.

MANSER, RUTH, AND FINLAN, LEONARD: *The Speaking Voice.* New York, Longmans, Green and Company, Inc., 1950.

Lesson 1

Sound: "ah" as in "father" (same as short "o")

Name: The laughing sound: Ha—Ha—Ha

Examples: father, army, honest

Description: Open the mouth wide as in a yawn. Let the sound roll
out. Keep the tongue relaxed at the bottom of the mouth.

Nonsense syllables

bäh	däh	täh	shäh

Words:

bomb	pot	hot	are

Sentences:

He *kno*cked at the *sho*p.
Jack *a*rgued with the *co*p.
Her d*o*ll lost an *a*rm.
T*o*m *sho*t his gun at the l*o*ck.
An h*o*nest man is h*a*rd to find.

Fig. 58. Happy, busy children are less likely to have trouble with their speech.

Lesson 2

Sound: "oh" as in "boat" (long "o")

Name: The "OK" sound

Examples: hoe, snow, own, go, oats

Description: Round the lips in a circle.
    Produce the same as "ah"

Nonsense syllables:

| pōh | fōh | kōh | zōh |

Words:

| go | toe | blow | show |

Sentences:

I don't want to go.
The pony stubbed his toe.
She won't answer the phone.
Her coat is yellow.
They wrote him a note.

Lesson 3

Sound: "uh" as in "cup" (short "u")

Name: The Indian sound: Ugh

Examples: gun, love, does

Description: Open the mouth slightly in a relaxed manner. Allow tone
    to flow out.

Nonsense syllables:

| dŭh | rŭh | pŭh | chŭh |

Words

| fun | done | come | cut |

Sentences:

The bum hit the puppy.
His uncle gave him money.
She put the buns in the oven.
Mother will shut the door.
There was mud in the gutter.

Lesson 4

Sound: "ă" as in "cat" (short "a")

Name: The billy goat sound: baaa

Examples: rat, laugh, nap

Description: Spread the lips a little more than for "ah." Open the mouth a little less wide.

Nonsense syllables:

dă	kă	ră	să

Words:

bad	rat	chat	hat

Sentences:

The bat was very mad.
The map was in the bag.
Black hats are back in style.
Jack began to shake the fan.
His dad is a wonderful man.

Lesson 5

Sound: "ē" as in "beet" (long "e")

Name: The squeaking door sound: Eeeee

Examples: me, leap, deed, thief, people

Description: With the teeth close together, spread the lips wide. Lift the tongue toward the roof of the mouth.

Nonsense syllables:

dēē	gēē	lēē	fēē	tēē

Words:

tree	sleep	three	these	deep

Sentences:

Please keep off my feet.
Give the key to the teacher
We like to read.
She hurt her knee.
The sea is very deep.

Lesson 6

Sound: "ĭ" as in "hit" (short "ĭ")

Name: The hiccough sound

Examples: mit, build, crypt

Description: Just like the "ē" except you let the mouth relax a little more. The sound is shorter than the "ē."

Nonsense syllables:

tĭh	pĭh	rĭh	dĭh	fĭh

Words:

bill	dip	kill	live	tick

Sentences:

There are six trees on the hill.
He did not put the lid away.
The ship was used for fishing.
I wish he would drink milk.
The king wrote the letter in ink.
He has a big spot on his lip.

Lesson 7

Sound: "ā" as in "cake" (long "a")

Name: The May-day sound.

Examples: day, break, mail, take

Description: Open the mouth a little more than for the "ĭ" sound, begin the sound and then let it slide toward the "ē" position.

Nonsense syllables:

bāy	fāy	tāy	chāy	jay

Words:

make	date	baby	sail	nāy

Sentences:

The rain fell near the lake.
They looked for it all day.
He stayed out very late.
The paper was a pale blue.
She made a raisin pie.

Lesson 8

Sound: "ĕ" as in "jet" (short "e")

Name: The old man's sound

Examples: bet, feather, said

Description: Open the mouth to a position about half way between that for "ā" and "ă." Extend the lips partially to the sides. The sound is shorter than for "ā."

Nonsense syllables:

dĕh	fĕh	gĕh	pĕh	zĕh

Words

beg	debt	fell	leg	tell

Sentences:

He met two men.
I guess I need help.
Mary's dress is bright red.
He wanted an egg for breakfast.
He said that he wanted to get to bed.

Lesson 9

Sound: "ōō" as in "you" (long double "o")
(with "y" becomes long "u")

Name: The surprise sound: oo-oo

Examples: two, shoe, grew, shoot

Description: Make as small a ring as possible with the lips. Force the air through.

Nonsense syllables:

bōō	fōō	hōō	lōō	wōō

Words:

blue	do	fool	cool	moon

Sentences:

His tooth hurts when he chews.
Do you know whose shoe it is?
Soup is very good at noon.
There are rules for eating food.
He wore his boots to the zoo.

Lesson 10

Sound: "ŏŏ" as in "book" (short double "o")

Name: The baby sound: ŏŏ

Examples: look, pull, could

Description: Like "ōō," but with lips more relaxed and the mouth a little more open. The sound is shorter than "ōō."

Nonsense:

dŏŏ	gŏŏ	chŏŏ	nŏŏ	kŏŏ

Words:

could	pull	brook	shook	wool

Sentences:

Look at that crook.
He would not carry the wood.
The cow stood on my foot.
You should not push the cook.
Cookies are good to put in your lunch.

Lesson 11

Sound: "aw" as in "saw"

Name: The refusing sound: naw

Examples: tall, fought, caught

Description: The mouth is a little less open than for short "ŏ." The lips are a little more rounded.

Nonsense syllables:

bâw	fâw	hâw	tâw	zâw

Words:

all	ought	wall	sauce	jaw

Sentences:

You must fall on the straw.
He taught her to play ball.
She thought she could draw.
He had gone to the office.
They fought on the lawn.

Lesson 12

Sound: "ī" as in "ice" (long "i")

Name: My sound: I

Examples: die, try, fight

Description: Begin with the "ä" sound (lesson 1) and slide toward the "ē" sound (lesson 5).

Nonsense syllables:

fī	jī	kī	rī	wī

Words:

eye	idea	fly	five	like

Sentences:

His *tie* was too *tight*.
We *might* go at *nine* o'clock.
My window was open *wide*.
He *tried* to *shine* the car.
The *child* sometimes *cried* at *night*.

Lesson 13

Sound: "ou" as in "house"

Name: The "hurt" sound: ouch!

Description: Begin with the "ä" sound (lesson 1) and slide toward the "ōō" sound (lesson 9).

Examples: couch, trout, pout

Nonsense syllables:

dou	fou	lou	pou	zou

Words:

about	cow	growl	now	vow

Sentences:

How can you pull *out* the flo*w*er?
You must *count* the h*ou*rs.
He sat *down* behind the *house*.
I *doubt* if he *found* the *cow*.
Don't sh*out* so *loud*.

Lesson 14

Sound: "oi" as in "boy"

Name: The "oily" sound.

Examples: joy, voice, choice

Description: Begin with the "aw" sound (lesson 11) and slide toward the "ē" sound (lesson 5).

Nonsense syllables:

doy	foy	loy	noy	voy

Words:

boil	joy	noise	poise	coin

Sentences:

He enjoys playing with his toys.

Boys often misuse their voices.

He tried to avoid the oysters.

Lloyd drove to Point Royal.

She joined her noisy friends.

Lesson 15

Sound: "P," the first sound in "pie"

Name: The motor-boat sound: putt-putt

Examples: paper, open, cup

Description: Press the lips together. Build up the air behind them. Puff the air out. If you put the back of the hand up in front of the mouth, you can feel the air. There is no tone; the vocal cords do not vibrate. Have the child watch you make the sound. Use the mirror to help in the study of the sound. In severe cases, the teacher may use her fingers to press the lips together so that the child can feel the necessary position. Be sure the sound comes out the mouth and is not exploded through the nose.

Nonsense syllables:

pā	pē	pī	pō	p$\overline{oo}$
āp	ēp	īp	ōp	$\overline{oo}$p
āpā	ēpē	īpī	ōpō	$\overline{oo}$p$\overline{oo}$

Words:

pay	pipe	pond	poor	put
apple	open	upon	paper	apron
pop	tap	keep	jump	ship

Sentences:

The *p*ig was aslee*p*.

*P*eople like to *p*ick u*p* *p*ennies.

*P*atty was busy mo*pp*ing the floor.

The to*p* fell into his la*p*.

You are su*pp*osed to sto*p*.

The hole was dee*p* in his *p*ocket.

Ha*pp*y children want to *p*lay games.

You must kee*p* your *p*aper.

You may o*p*en the *p*ackage.

The *p*arrot was his *p*et.

Lesson 16

Sound: "b," the beginning sound in "baby"

Name: The bubble sound: buh, buh

Examples: ball, rabbit, Bob

Description: Just like "p" (lesson 15) except there is tone from the vocal cords. The sound is voiced.

Nonsense syllables:

bā	bē	bī	bō	bo͞o
āb	ēb	īb	ōb	o͞ob
ābā	ēbē	ībī	ōbō	o͞obo͞o

Words:

ball	bear	book	boat	boy
table	above	rabbit	number	cupboard
Bob	cab	bib	knob	tub
blow	blood	blaze	blank	blue
brag	brake	bread	brief	brown

Sentences:

The *b*ed was *b*roken.

The *b*oy was very *b*rave.

The *b*ee flew into a *b*ottle.

The ro*bb*er fell over the *b*room.

A *b*ulldog tried to *b*ite him.

He was *b*usy with his *b*utterfly net.

Mr. *B*utler asked him to *b*uy it.

*B*ring your notes to the *b*usiness meeting.

The *b*lanket is almost *b*lack.

The *b*omber flew below the *b*ank of clouds.

Lesson 17

Sound: "m," the beginning sound in "mama"

Name: The "humming" sound

Examples: mouse, hammer, grim

Directions: Put the lips together as with "p" and "b." Let the air
stream flow out through the nose while the lips remain closed. The
vocal cords produce tone.

Nonsense syllables:

mā	mē	mī	mō	m$\overline{oo}$
ām	ēm	īm	ōm	$\overline{oo}$m
āmā	ēmē	īmī	ōmō	$\overline{oo}$m$\overline{oo}$

Words:

man	must	mouse	meet	might
hammer	coming	among	lemon	famous
them	seem	dime	home	gum

Sentences:

Tom wants mush all the time.

Let's meet at my house.

Her lamp is larger than mine.

The man was mean to the mouse.

His mother is named Mary.

Many animals have small feet.

The mop was in the middle of the mess.

The farmer had an empty pail.

It was time for the morning meal.

I like to swim during the summer.

Lesson 18

Sound: "t," the beginning sound in "top"

Name: The "tick-tock" sound

Examples: time, water, boat

Directions: Place the tip of the tongue against the gum ridge just back
of the upper front teeth. Stop the air stream. Then move the tongue
downward quickly and allow the air to explode out the mouth.
There is no vibration of the vocal cords. The sound is voiceless.
In severe cases it is sometimes necessary for the child to hold his
nose while he learns to send the air out the mouth in producing "t."

Nonsense syllables:

tā	tē	tī	tō	to͞o
āt	ēt	īt	ōt	o͞ot
ātā	ētē	ītī	ōtō	o͞oto͞o

Words:

take	tip	tree	time	tooth
water	butter	letter	bitter	bottle
but	eat	coat	lot	heart

Sentences:

Tom sat at the table.
The tack was on top of the tent.
The tall man told his story.
The cat ran after the light.
She tore the mitten.
He talked on the telephone.
Timmy wanted to sell his tricycle.
She got dirt on her feet.
Lots of people went to the party.
His sister spent ten cents.

Lesson 19

Sound: "d," the first sound in "dog"

Name: The "drip" sound: dd-dd-ddd

Examples: dog, hidden, bed

Directions: Same as "t" except that the vocal cords vibrate. There is tone. If the tongue is slow, exercises for movement of the tongue are valuable.

Nonsense syllables:

dā	dē	dī	dō	do͞o
ād	ēd	īd	ōd	o͞od
ādā	ēdē	īdī	ōdō	o͞odo͞o

Words:

day	down	dime	deer	dinner
candy	today	sudden	burden	body
good	stood	bed	hand	need

Sentences:

He ha*d* to run un*d*er the be*d*.

He opene*d* the *d*oor too har*d*.

*D*on hit his hea*d* on the win*d*ow.

They coul*d* lan*d* in the san*d*.

He turne*d* the ra*d*io very lou*d*.

She hi*d* the can*d*y in the cupboar*d*.

I nee*d* a *d*ime for the san*d*wich.

She wante*d* a re*d* *d*ress.

*D*ick *d*roppe*d* the see*d*s.

The chil*d*ren ate the pu*dd*ing.

Lesson 20

Sound: "n," the beginning sound in "no"

Name: The "airplane" sound: "nnnnn"

Examples: night, dinner, sun

Directions: Same position as for "t" and "d." Instead of exploding the air through the mouth, allow it to flow through the nose. Keep the tip of the tongue against the gum ridge.

Nonsense syllables:

nā	nē	nī	nō	noō
ān	ēn	īn	ōn	oōn
ānā	ēnē	īnī	ōnō	oōnoō

Words:

not	night	name	noise	nice
funny	pony	dinner	sense	tent
brown	fine	train	green	men

Sentences:

He ra*n* i*n*to the ma*n*.

*N*ever be late for di*nn*er.

We have lu*n*ch at *n*oon.

She ope*n*ed the ove*n* door.

He wa*n*ted a doze*n n*eckties.

The su*n* was shi*n*ing in *N*ebraska.

His o*n*ly cha*n*ce was to ru*n*.

The trai*n* was te*n* mi*n*utes late.

The a*n*imal made a *n*oise.

The butto*n* on his coat was broke*n*.

Lesson 21

Sound: "k," the first sound in "king"

Name: The "clicking" sound

Examples: cop, bacon, cook

Directions: Stop the air stream by raising the back of the tongue. Let the tongue drop quickly, allowing the air to explode through the mouth. If necessary, hold the nose so that the sound doesn't escape through the nose. It is helpful to touch the front of the throat slightly to indicate the approximate position of the sound. There is no vibration; the sound is voiceless. Let the child imagine that he is coughing up some obstruction (such as a bone) in the throat.

Nonsense syllables:

kā	kē	kī	kō	k͞oo
āk	ēk	īk	ōk	͞ook
ākā	ēkē	īkī	ōkō	͞ook͞oo

Words:

can	come	count	keep	cough
because	cocoa	second	making	picnic
look	milk	cook	black	luck

Sentences:

Jack ate the cake.

Come into the kitchen for coffee.

The cat caught the mouse.

Can you count the candles?

Carl tried to kick the cow.

Keep the crumbs off the book.

She likes pretty clothes.

The class cleaned out the closet.

He took the car to the cabin.

The kite was lost in the sky.

Lesson 22

Sound: "g," the beginning sound in "go"

Name: The "water from a jug" sound: gugugugu

Examples: gone, sugar, bug

Directions: Same as "k" except that the vocal cords vibrate. Again the tip of the finger may be placed on the "button" at the front of the throat to indicate the position of the sound.

Nonsense syllables:

gā	gē	gī	gō	gōō
āg	ēg	īg	ōg	ōōg
āgā	ēgē	īgī	ōgō	ōōgōō

Words:

good	goat	gone	green	gun
ago	sugar	wagon	again	began
egg	leg	dog	pig	bug
glass	glad	glow	great	grape

Sentences:

The girl had gone.

The geese ate the grain.

It began to rain on the wagon.

Mr. Green smoked a big cigar.

Grace took the flag away.

He forgot to get his glasses.

The dog grew and grew.

The cigarette fell on the ground.

He was glum about his grades.

She gave him some gravy.

Lesson 23

Sound: "ng," the ending sound in "ring"

Name: The "ing" sound

Examples: bank, monkey, sing

Description: Use the same position as for "k" and "g." Allow the air to flow out through the nose.

Nonsense syllables:

ngā	ngē	ngī	ngō	ngōō
āng	ēng	īng	ōng	ōōng
āngā	ēngē	īngī	ōngō	ōōngōō

Words:

finger	donkey	banker
singer	single	blank

Sentences:

The king was strong.

Everything went wrong.

His finger was very long.

The monkey was going fast.

Bring the singer along.

Lesson 24

Sound: "w," the beginning sound in "water"

Name: The wind sound.

Examples: wait, window, away

Description: Make the position for the "ōō" sound (lesson 9); lips protruded and made into a small circle. The vocal cords vibrate as the mouth goes into the position for the following vowel.

Nonsense syllables:

wā	wē	wī	wō	wōō
āwā	ēwē	īwī	ōwō	ōōwōō

Words:

we	will	won	work	weed
away	between	always	awake	unwind

Sentences:

They *w*ere on their *w*ay home.

He *w*ent to the *w*edding.

His *w*allet got *w*et.

He *w*anted to eat the sand*w*ich.

She *w*ished to be a *w*itch.

Lesson 25

Sound: "wh," the beginning sound in "white"

Name: The "whistle" sound

Examples: when, whale, somewhere

Description: Make the position for "w." Blow a little air out before the vocal cords start to vibrate. This sound is not necessary for intelligible speech; better speakers use it.

Nonsense syllables

whā	whē	whī	whō	whōō
āwhā	ēwhē	īwhī	ōwhō	ōōwhōō

Words:

wheel	while	when	whip	whale

Sentences:

*Wh*ere is the *wh*irlpool?

*Wh*en did the bob*wh*ite sing?

*Wh*y did the dog *wh*ine?

*Wh*at is the price of *wh*eat?

*Wh*ich one of you was *wh*ispering?

Lesson 26

Sound: "h," the beginning sound in "hat"

Name: The "panting" sound

Examples: happy, hero, home

Directions: Force a small amount of air through the mouth before beginning the following vowel. The "h" is merely an approach to a vowel.

Nonsense syllables:

hā	hē	hī	hō	hōō
āhā	ēhē	īhī	ōhō	ōōhōō

Words:

how	hello	her	hand	horse

Sentences:

He was happy to help.
She hid in the lighthouse.
The horse was very hungry.
Harry hurried to help.
Helen hid behind her hat.

Lesson 27

Sound: "th," the beginning sound in "thing"

Name: The "thinking" sound

Examples: thin, birthday, eighth

Description: Place the tip of the tongue between the front teeth. Force air out between the tongue and the upper teeth. There is no tone.

Nonsense syllables:

thā	thē	thī	thō	thōō
āthā	ēthē	īthī	ōthō	ōōthōō
āth	ēth	īth	ōth	ōōth

Words:

thank	think	three	thumb	thin
bath	teeth	truth	Ruth	month

Sentences:

> *Th*ree boys *th*ought of it.
>
> I *th*ink it is too *th*ick.
>
> The baby puts every*th*ing in his mou*th*.
>
> Ru*th* is in the four*th* grade.
>
> The too*th*brush is in the ba*th*room.
>
> The au*th*or was tru*th*ful.
>
> Nor*th* is the opposite of sou*th*.
>
> Bo*th* of us caught the *th*ief.
>
> The pa*th* goes into the *th*ick woods.
>
> A *th*ousand men faced dea*th*.

Lesson 28

Sound: "th," the beginning sound in "these"

Name: The "vacuum cleaner" sound

Examples: those, other, with

Description: The same as "th" except that the vocal cords vibrate.

Nonsense syllables:

thā	thē	thī	thō	thōo
āth	ēth	īth	ōth	ōoth
āthā	ēthē	īthī	ōthō	ōothōo

Words:

they	that	them	thus	those
another	father	breathe	bathed	clothed

Sentences:

> *Th*ere was a fea*th*er in it.
>
> All the bro*th*ers were toge*th*er.
>
> The bad wea*th*er was a bo*th*er.
>
> *Th*is man went wi*th* us.
>
> Her mo*th*er told her to ba*th*e.

Lesson 29

Sound: "f," the beginning sound in "fish"

Name: The "angry cat" sound

Examples: fine, coffee, laugh

Description: Place the lower lip against the upper front teeth. Force the air out between them. There is no tone. Use of the mirror is good in establishing the position. Have the child watch and listen as you make the sound. He may substitute "t," "p," or "s" for the "f."

Nonsense syllables:

fā	fē	fī	fō	fōō
āf	ēf	īf	ōf	ōōf
āfā	ēfē	īfī	ōfō	ōōfōō

Words:

fine	fat	feel	funny	found
after	before	coffee	sofa	careful
if	leaf	safe	thief	off

Courtesy of Morrison Center for Rehabilitation.

Fig. 59. Matching pictures adds visual clues to the
auditory ones.

Sentences:
His *f*ather made a big *f*uss.
He had enou*gh* money *f*or the kni*f*e.
The thie*f* was very *f*ierce.
That makes me *f*eel like a *f*ool.
The *f*ox got there *f*irst.
Hal*f* of thirty is *f*i*f*teen.
The lea*f* *f*ell o*ff* the tree.
The gold*f*ish acts very funny.
The cal*f* has a white *f*ace.
*F*ruit is better than *f*ried *f*ood.

Lesson 30

Sound: "v," the beginning sound in "very"
Name: The "electric fan" sound: "vvvvvv"
Examples: vine, oven, of
Description: The same as "f" with the addition of tone. If necessary
  the child can be instructed to bite on his lower lip or to press the
  lower lip against the edge of the upper teeth with his finger. He
  may substitute "b" for "v."

Nonsense syllables:

vā	vē	vī	vō	vo͞o
āv	ēv	īv	ōv	o͞ov
āvā	ēvē	īvī	ōvō	o͞ovo͞o

Words:

vine	vase	view	vote	violin
even	ever	over	seven	never
five	glove	stove	give	have

Sentences:
Vera has a soft *v*oice.
He had se*v*en days of *v*acation.
I lo*v*e the *v*iew from the hill.
They mo*v*ed to the *v*alley.
He spilled gra*v*y on his *v*est.
Let's dri*v*e to the *v*illage.
He tried to sa*v*e Victor.
She ga*v*e him a *v*alentine.
She wants to tra*v*el to Virginia.
The sto*v*e was *v*ery hot.

Lesson 31

Sound: "sh," the beginning sound in "show"

Name: The "shushing" sound

Description: The teeth are separated slightly. The lips are protruded and rounded a little. The sides of the tongue are drawn up against the teeth at the sides of the mouth. The air stream is forced out through the mouth. There is no tone. The child may substitute "t," "s," or "th" for the "sh" sound.

Nonsense syllables:

shā	shē	shī	shō	shōō
āsh	ēsh	īsh	ōsh	ōōsh
āshā	ēshē	īshī	ōshō	ōōshōō

Words:

she	shop	shout	shut	shore
ocean	fishing	push	fresh	dish

Sentences:

I wish I could go fishing.
The sheep were near the ocean.
You should always wash your face.
The ship has a big shadow.
He shook the water off his shirt.
She tried to finish the washing.
He wore black shoes to the show.
Sheila ate a dish of radishes.
A sharp stick hit his shin.
Shredded wheat is sure to please.

Lesson 32

Sound: "zh," the middle consonant in "measure"

Name: The "drunk" sound

Examples: pleasure, decision, usual

Description: The same as "sh" with the addition of tone. The child may substitute "d," "j," or "z" for it.

Nonsense syllables:

zhā	zhē	zhī	zhō	zho͞o
āzh	ēzh	īzh	ōzh	o͞ozh
āzhā	ēzhē	īzhī	ōzhō	o͞ozho͞o

Words:

azure	garage	treasure	usual	vision

Sentences:

They measured the rug.

The treasure was lost.

It was a happy occasion.

He paid the usual amount.

The trip was a real pleasure.

Lesson 33

Sound: "y," the beginning sound in "yes"

Name: The "yipping" sound

Examples: young, yellow, million

Description: Place the tongue and lips in the position for "ē" (lesson 5). Then begin tone and slide into the position for the following vowel. The child may omit the sound or substitute "w" for it.

Nonsense syllables:

yā	yē	yī	yō	yo͞o
āyā	ēyē	īyī	ōyō	o͞oyo͞o

Words:

year	yet	yell	beyond	loyal

Sentences:

You may eat the onion.

A new year began yesterday.

Your friend is very young.

Our yacht is painted yellow.

What is the value of a million pounds?

Lesson 34

Sound: "ch," the beginning sound in "cheese"

Name: The "choo-choo train" sound

Examples: child, teacher, beach

Description: "Ch" is a blend of two sounds: "t" and "sh." They are pronounced so closely together that they emerge as one sound. If the child is older, you may separate the two sounds and then combine them again. Care must be taken that the sound is exploded through the mouth and not through the nose. He may need to hold his nose until the correct direction of the air is established. There is no tone. The child usually substitutes "t," "sh," or "k" for the "ch" sound.

Nonsense syllables:

chā	chē	chī	chō	chōō
āch	ēch	īch	ōch	ōōch
āchā	ēchē	īchī	ōchō	ōōchōō

Words:

chair	chew	China	chose	child
teacher	kitchen	rich	each	watch

Fig. 60. "Choo-choo, choo-choo," says the train.

Sentences:

The cat *ch*ased the mouse into the *ch*ur*ch*.
We ate lun*ch* on the ben*ch*.
You shouldn't *ch*ew on mat*ch*es.
He eats a *ch*erry ea*ch* day.
His spee*ch* was mu*ch* improved.
The *ch*ildren went to the bea*ch*.
The bran*ch* fell in the or*ch*ard.
*Ch*arlie was the ri*ch*est man in town.
I like to wa*tch* the tennis ma*tch*.
Pea*ch* pie is very ri*ch*.

Lesson 35

Sound: "j," the beginning sound in "jump"

Name: The "jug" sound

Examples: jelly, magic, orange

Description: Same as "ch" with tone added. "J" is the blending of
 "d" and "zh." The child may substitute "d" or "zh" for "j."

Nonsense syllables:

jā	jē	jī	jō	jo͞o
āj	ēj	īj	ōj	o͞oj
ājā	ējē	ījī	ōjō	o͞ojo͞o

Words:

jam	jelly	joke	jug	juice
pigeon	imagine	cage	large	age

Sentences:

A large dog *j*umped at him.
The oranges were not *j*uicy.
Roy Rogers was on the e*dg*e of the cliff.
They put the *j*anitor in *j*ail.
His ma*g*ic trick was a *j*oke.
*J*ane ran over the bri*dg*e.
He was *j*ust on pa*g*e seven.
He left his *j*acket at the lo*dg*e.
He *ch*anged the water in the en*g*ine.
*J*ames put the bird in the ca*g*e.

Lesson 36

Sound: "s," the beginning sound in "see"

Name: The "snake" sound

Examples: see, gasoline, pass

Description: Touch the front teeth together, hiding the tongue behind them. Raise the sides of the tongue forming a small groove in the middle. Force air between the central front teeth. It is often helpful to start the "s" from the "t" position (lesson 18). Don't produce a "t" sound except for practice—as, "ts." Then eliminate the "t" and retain the "s" sound. Mirror work is good for establishing the teeth closed, tongue back position.

Nonsense syllables:

sā	sē	sī	sō	so͞o
ās	ēs	īs	ōs	o͞os
āsā	ēsē	īsī	ōsō	o͞oso͞o

Words:

saw	sing	sleep	soon	stay
faster	lesson	missing	baseball	possible
dress	loss	nice	this	miss
spade	small	street	splash	school
box	maps	horse	laughs	months

Sentences:

I see the brown mouse.

Sam didn't like the soup.

It stopped snowing about noon.

Her voice is too soft.

I like the study of history.

Christmas will soon be here.

Let's all sing a few songs.

The time seems to go very slowly.

The trip took six gallons of gasoline.

The small boy sat on the coats.

Lesson 37

Sound: "z," the beginning sound in "zoo"

Name: The "buzzing" sound

Examples: zoo, easy, rose

Directions: The same as "s" with the addition of tone.

Nonsense syllables:

zā	zē	zī	zō	zōō
āzā	ēzē	īzī	ōzō	ōōzōō
āz	ēz	īz	ōz	ōōz

Words:

zero	zone	busy	cousin	lazy
has	please	use	because	was

Sentences:

We made a visit to the zoo.

The zebra was very lazy.

He has a dozen pairs of shoes.

My cousin is crazy about music.

Those colors are very pleasing.

Zeke won the first prize.

The closet door was closed.

Please tell me the big surprise.

It is easy to wash your hands.

The bee buzzed around the roses.

Lesson 38

Sound: "l," the beginning sound in "light"

Name: The "singing" sound: la, la, la

Examples: lamp, hello, ball

Description: Place the tip of the tongue against the roof of the mouth about an inch back of the upper teeth. Begin the production of tone, allowing the air stream to pass around both sides of the tongue. Then the tongue is moved downward to produce the following vowel. If a heavy "l" sound is being produced at the end of a word, as in "bottle," the tongue tip remains against the roof of the mouth. Have the child watch you make the sound. Mirror practice is also good. Singing simple melodies with "la-la" instead of words is useful. The size of the mouth opening depends upon the vowels which follows "l"; it is probably easiest to begin with "ŏ" or "ī," as in "lot" or "life."

Nonsense syllables:

lā	lē	lī	lō	lōō
ālā	ēlē	īlī	ōlō	ōōlōō
āl	ēl	īl	ōl	ōōl

Words:

lake	let	like	look	love
belong	only	hello	yellow	pillow
all	rule	tail	little	people
black	clean	glad	fly	play
elm	twelve	help	milk	world

Sentences:

I *l*ike to eat my *l*unch.

He *l*eft his hat on the *l*edge.

He found an app*l*e under the *l*adder.

*L*arry turned on the *l*ight.

The *l*eaf is a*l*most b*l*ack.

My schoo*l* is on top of the hi*ll*.

I wi*ll* fo*ll*ow you on my bicyc*l*e.

His *l*eg was b*l*eeding very bad*l*y.

The g*l*ass was fu*ll* of *l*iquid.

Peop*l*e *l*ike to *l*ive in Ca*l*ifornia.

Lesson 39

Sound: "r," the beginning sound in "rose"

Name: The "growling" sound

Examples: read, tomorrow

Description: Raise the sides of the tongue against the upper back teeth. Draw the tip of the tongue toward the back of the mouth. There is tone throughout. The shape of the lips depend upon the vowel which follows "r." To avoid a "w" sound, spread the lips slightly so that they do not become too rounded. One may push the corners of the mouth back with the finger tips. The usual substitution for "r" is "w."

Nonsense syllables:

rā	rē	rī	rō	rōo̅
ārā	ērē	īrī	ōrō	o̅oro̅o̅

Words:

rat	rabbit	room	rose	rich
around	story	bread	cross	drink
froze	gray	price	three	street

Sentences:

The *r*ain fell on the *r*oof.

The *r*ed house is very p*r*etty.

*R*obert has t*r*ouble with *r*eading.

He was w*r*ong about the *r*ules.

The *r*ope was lying in the st*r*eet.

His b*r*other hit him with a b*r*oom.

The p*r*ice of f*r*uit is high.

The c*r*ow landed in the t*r*ee.

He w*r*ote a letter to his *r*ich uncle.

The boys are *r*ough on the play*gr*ound.

Lesson 40

Sound: "er," the ending sound in "mother"

Name: The "crowing rooster" sound: er, er, er

Examples: bird, church, sister

Description: Very similar to "r," except that the tongue is more relaxed, and the tip is farther forward. It is used in General American
speech but is slighted or modified in both Eastern and Southern
speech.

Nonsense syllables:

erā	erē	erī	erō	er$\overline{oo}$
āer	ēer	īer	ōer	$\overline{oo}$er

Words:

earth	early	bird	dirt	curl
curve	firm	fourth	learn	fork

Sentences:

Mary's moth*er* washed the c*ur*tains.

I know wh*er*e I put the lett*er*.

The g*ir*l had a blue sk*ir*t.

He h*ear*d the bell from the ch*ur*ch.

A b*ear* was caught n*ear* our house.

He spilled wat*er* on the chai*r*.

The h*or*se was in the b*ar*n.

She ate the c*or*n with a f*or*k.

Your sist*er* is old*er* than Billy.

I like summ*er* mo*r*e than wint*er*.

INDEX

This Book

SPEECH CORRECTION AT HOME

By

MORRIS VAL JONES, Ph.D.

was set and printed by The Hart Printing Company of St. Louis, Missouri. It was bound by the Becktold Company of St. Louis, Missouri. The engravings were made by The Capitol Engraving and Electrotype Company of Springfield, Illinois. The page trim size is 6 x 9 inches. The type page is 26 x 43 picas. The type face is Caledonia, set 10 point on 13 point. The text paper is 70 lb. Trufect. The cover is Bancroft's Oxford 6415 (Maroon).

With THOMAS BOOKS careful attention is given to all details of manufacturing and design. It is the publisher's desire to present books that are satisfactory as to their physical qualities and artistic possibilities and appropriate for their particular use. THOMAS BOOKS will be true to those laws of quality that assure a good name and good will.